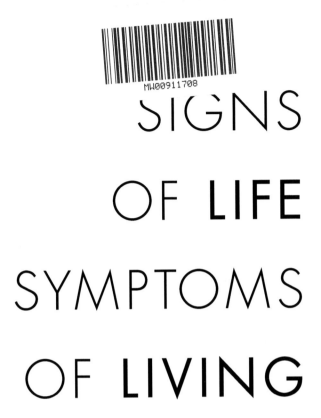

# SIGNS

# OF **LIFE**

# SYMPTOMS

# OF **LIVING**

CHANCE WILLIAMS, M.D.

# SIGNS

# OF **LIFE**

# SYMPTOMS

# OF **LIVING**

Rediscovering
the Heart of a Man

Tate Publishing & Enterprises

Published by Tate Publishing & Enterprises, LLC
127 E. Trade Center Terrace | Mustang, Oklahoma 73064 USA
1.888.361.9473 | www.tatepublishing.com

Tate Publishing is committed to excellence in the publishing industry. The company reflects the philosophy established by the founders, based on Psalm 68:11,
*"The Lord gave the word and great was the company of those who published it."*

Book design copyright © 2010 by Tate Publishing, LLC. All rights reserved.
*Cover design by Amber Gulilat*
*Interior design by Nathan Harmony*

Published in the United States of America

ISBN: 978-1-61663-704-0
1. Religion / Christian Life / Spiritual Growth
2. Religion / Christian Life / Personal Growth
10.08.24

# ᨸ TABLE OF CONTENTS ᨸ

# INTRODUCTION

> To know God, this is eternal life; this is the purpose for which we are and were created.
> —A.W. Tozer

For the last ten years, I have worked as a family practice physician. Over that period of time, there has rarely been a day that I did not encounter someone suffering from heart disease in its various forms and presentations. The general public has become more keenly aware of heart disease and its impact on men and women. The pharmaceutical industry has brought information to the forefront through TV advertisements discussing various drugs and their potential impact on reducing your personal risk of heart attack or recurrence of a heart event. Every year, statistical data is presented in lecture halls around the country discussing heart disease, as it continues to be a leading cause of death of men and women of all ages, not only in the US but worldwide. So if such a dangerous set of circumstances places us at risk for heart disease, why do we not listen? Why do we not heed the warnings from our doctors to quit drinking, quit smoking, watch our diets, and get some exercise? Why are those New Year's resolutions so hard to stick to? Why do men and women continue to be picked off, one by one, having disastrous effects on their families, their churches, their cultures?

As a follower of Christ, I have seen a similar illness in the lives of men of all ages. Heart disease affects them in their day-to-day lives and has very serious consequences in the lives of their families, their church, and also on their eternity. I'm not talking about physical consequences from an actual event such as a heart attack. Rather, I'm talking about a series of events that cause men to lose heart and walk away from God, their families, their church, and their brotherhood. Yes, there are physical consequences seen in their lives at times, but ultimately, there are spiritual consequences that play out as a result of having a heart so diseased and robbed of the nurturing care needed to sustain life.

Just take a look around you. If you have been in the faith community at all, you have seen many of these men dropping off the radar. It starts with maybe just skipping a men's small group. They just could not find the time. But that was well after they had dropped out of meeting with God in their quiet times each day. Before long, they are no longer in church. They may eventually drop out of their families and eventually drop out of life.

Rarely does someone die of heart disease without warning. Usually there are signs and symptoms of an impending event about to take place. The story of our lives—how we eat, how much we exercise, what meds we take regularly, and how we take care of our bodies can be a dead giveaway of what future consequences may be in store. And is it not the very same with our hearts on a spiritual level?

The choices we make will determine the life we experience here on this earth and for all eternity. Our story with God—how we feed our spirit; how much we exercise our faith; how we discipline our bodies, minds, and spirits to seek after God; and whether we allow interaction with others in our life of faith—help to determine future spiritual consequences. So why do we not heed the warnings when our heart is about to fail within us?

What obstacles keep you from truly finding life? Is it power, possessions, fear of failure, present comforts, change, or past events? What is the truth about what we know? Everyone was born—once. And everyone will die. We came into the world naked and unclothed. We will depart it leaving our earthly clothes and possessions behind. From the dust of the earth we were born (see Genesis 2). To the dust of the earth we will return. Yet our souls will remain and live on into eternity.

When our heart stops beating in our chest, we will be transported into the presence of God, but until our hearts stop, everything we do in this body has temporal and eternal significance. The choices we make in how we lead our lives impacts those around us—our wives, our children, our families, our church, and unbelievers—and it impacts our eternal reward in heaven.

So how is your heart? Are you guarding it well? Are you equipped to step into the role God has for you as his son, as a husband, as a father, as a brother? We must take time to consider well the ways of our hearts, to examine our lives, to have a deep soul to soul discussion as brothers, and to sharpen one another—as iron sharpens iron—for the sake of and the glory of Christ. To begin, we have to understand that he who created us has a very specific purpose for our life.

Have you ever actually sat down and thought about the human body? It is amazingly complex in its every function and amazingly resilient to ward off disease, illness, and injury in this world that wages against our very existence. Yet why would God take the time to develop the intricacies of our anatomy, the pathways of understanding to our physiology, the idiosyncrasies of our personality? Did he create us to be mere displays of his awesome talents and to shadow his likeness? What sets us apart from all the rest of creation? At the core of our being in our very soul, how has God set us apart?

To answer the last question, we need to focus our attention on the heart. The Latin word for heart is *cor*. So a study of the heart is a study at the very core of who we are. What does God say about the heart? He tells us in Proverbs 4:23, "Above all else, guard your heart, for it is the wellspring of life." It seems like such a simple statement, such an easy directive, yet we do not have to look very far to see what happens when we are careless and lax about the care of our hearts.

How does Proverbs 4:23 strike you at first glance? Does it seem like a simple task? Would it be easy to overlook? Do you get a sense of how God views your heart? Was it merely a passing statement made by him in the middle of a book of suggestions? No. Never. It is a call to action, the mission of missions, and a declaration of war. Guard your heart. The source of all you will ever become depends upon it.

1 Peter 5:8 reminds us of the battle for our hearts, "Be self-controlled and alert. Your enemy the devil prowls around like a roaring lion looking for someone to devour." And Jesus asks us in Matthew 16:26, "What good will it be for a man if he gains the whole world, yet forfeits his soul? Or what can a man give in exchange for his soul?" Look again at the parable of the sower in Matthew 13.

> A farmer went out to sow his seed. As he was scattering the seed, some fell along the path, and the birds came and ate it up. Some fell on rocky places, where it did not have much soil. It sprang up quickly because the soil was shallow. But when the sun came up, the plants were scorched, and they withered because they had no root. Other seed fell among thorns, which grew up and choked the plants. Still other seed fell on good soil, where it produced a crop—a hundred, sixty or thirty times what was sown. He who has ears let him hear.
>
> The knowledge of the secrets of the kingdom of heaven has been given to you, but not to them. Whoever has will be given more, and he will have an abundance. Whoever does not have, even what he has will be taken from him.
>
> But blessed are your eyes because they see, and your ears because they hear. Listen then to what the parable of the sower means: when anyone hears the message about the kingdom and does not un-

derstand it, the evil one comes and snatches away
what was sown in his heart. This is the seed sown
along the path. The one who received the seed that
fell on rocky places is the man who hears the word
and at once receives it with joy. But since he has no
root, he lasts only a short time. When trouble or
persecution comes because of the word, he quickly
falls away. The one who received the seed that fell
among the thorns is the man who hears the word,
but the worries of this life and the deceitfulness of
wealth choke it, making it unfruitful. But the one
who received the seed that fell on good soil is the
man who hears the word and understands it. He
produces a crop, yielding a hundred, sixty or thirty
times what was sown.

Matthew 13:1–9, 11–12, 16–23 (NIV)

Christ Jesus knows our hearts. He knows what is within a
man, the potential for amazing good and the potential for
disaster. He is able to pinpoint exactly the heart's response
to the Word of God. But did you catch his exhortation
to the disciples in the lines between the story of the parable. He is encouraging them to never give up. Something
awesome is alive in them, and it has enormous potential.
The knowledge of the secrets of the kingdom of heaven
has been given unto them and to us.

It is not by accident that God calls us to guard our
heart. The Creator knows just what is in the heart and
what it is capable of. We look to the heart to provide a
vital source of life sustaining power. Rarely will you ever be
examined by a doctor without him or her listening to your

heart. Never will you hear from God without it impacting on your heart. As men, we need to look at the importance of heart health before God. If he tells us to guard our hearts for they are the wellspring—*the source, the origin*—of life. Should we not take the time to get checked out with the Great Physician? We need to hear from him and see what he sees in our hearts. We need to gauge our lives according to his principles. We might need to make some lifestyle changes for the sake of our spiritual health and to learn the strength and the resolve that he has placed within each of our hearts to live as men, as husbands, fathers, and sons. We must learn to live again as his Spirit penetrates our hearts with life-sustaining breath.

The objective of this time together is to impact your life at the core. I hope you are able to encounter God, to get more than a glimpse of how he views your heart and how he wants to take you to deeper levels in your walk with him and your understanding of him. I want you to experience life, to find healing, to draw near to God, and to dream again.

# BLOOD PRESSURE
## Awkward Tensions of Life

What a name for a chapter in a book, eh? So are you intrigued, wanting to read on just to find out what in the world your blood pressure has to do with anything at all spiritual? Well, I will get to that in a minute. I wouldn't be surprised if this is not your first discussion of the day about blood pressure. You were probably talking with your buddy at the donut shop this morning about his or your recent visit to the doctor's office. "Why do they have to pump that blasted blood pressure cuff up to the point that it feels like my arm is about to explode and drop off? It's worse than a bad Boy Scout tourniquet. Oh, and if they have to pump it up a second time and go even higher, that's never a good sign. And by all means, don't try to talk to the nurse while she is checking your blood pressure. All she can hear is your muffled voice and not your heart beat! So you guessed it! She's going to crank it up there again!"

Much as a barometer is a sign of a change in the

weather when a storm is brewing, so your blood pressure is also a gauge of heart health, and unfortunately, it can also be a sign of things to come—especially without intervention. When it comes to matters of the heart spiritually, how are we to measure our blood pressure? Can we recognize when the pressure is getting too high? What is God's prescription for the ailing heart? Blood pressure represents the degree to which we are really alive—the awkward tension of life. You may want to think of it as balance or a state of equilibrium, but it is that sphere in which we are truly functioning, interacting, and healthy.

We live in a physical world. We have needs, and as men, we strive to meet the needs of our families through pouring ourselves into work—sacrificing time, expending energy, and spending long days away from those for whom we are wanting to provide. We try to get ahead, but typically just end up paying down debts and never really invest in a future inheritance. Life boils down to shelter, food, comfort, and a warm bed to sleep in at night—hopefully with someone to share it all with. The pace is tremendous, and we struggle to keep up. Everyone else seems to have it all—the nice house, the new car, the perfect marriage, the best kids.

## Do We Recognize the Signs of a Healthy Versus an Ailing Heart?

According to Proverbs 14, "A heart at peace gives life to the body, but envy rots the bones" (Proverbs 14:30, NIV). What does a heart at peace look like? It sounds very inviting, like a hike up a mountain to a pristinely clear lake full of rainbow trout. You hear nothing but the sounds of nature in the air: the wind blowing through the aspen, a few song birds passing by talking to each other, and the sounds of a waterfall not far off. Can you imagine sharing that with your son on his first-ever hike into the woods with his fly-fishing rod in tow? Oh, the excitement, the joy, the imagination, the awe of it all around him. And let's not forget the chatter of a boy who feels like a man, hanging out with his dad, facing nature, and looking forward to the big catch. Does that look like peace? Does that sound like life?

Let's compare that with what many of us face every day. The cell phone rings, you're called back to work yet again, and your dinner is left on the table. The time you promised to spend with your kids out throwing the ball is gone; you've got to perform to impress your boss. The debts are heavy; you're living beyond your means and borrowing against your future. You speak those familiar words, always telling your kids there will be time this weekend or the next, and then we'll take that trip to the mountains. Just like the one that didn't happen last year.

And what is all this working and striving and straining for? Let's just cut to the chase and call it what it is— envy! That feeling of discontent and resentment wells up inside once again because you cannot seem to gain what everyone else seems to have or measure up to the world's expectations. The kingdom of self you have created is caving in on you. You are striving to keep up the appearance, but there are more leaks in the dam than you have fingers and toes. Your marrow is worn out. You've pushed too far.

Your energy is sapped. What is (was) most important to you gets only the leftovers. The desire for more has failed you. Envy rots the bones.

Take a closer look at the second part of the verse again. What happens to the heart? When you make it to the end of the rat race and are at the finish line there with your rotten bones, your heart is still alive. It's beating in your chest, following the design of the Master, waiting for you to choose a different path, and giving you a second chance to start anew. Until your heart stops, there is always an opportunity for change, for redemption, for renewal of all things.

> "I will be found by you," declares the Lord, "and will bring you back from captivity."
>
> Jeremiah 29:14 (NIV)

Allow the Creator to captivate you. Free yourself from distracting allures and desires. Catch a glimpse of God's prescription plan for all that ails you. Find out who you are, put off envy with confidence and what do you find left? *Peace.* And what does peace bring? *Life!*

## What Is God's Prescription for the Ailing Heart?

In Psalm 37, David encourages us to "trust in the Lord," "delight [ourselves] in the Lord," "commit [our ways] to the Lord," "hope in the Lord," and "wait patiently for him" (vs. 3–5, 7,9). What are the results? You will be given "the desires of your heart," you will "inherit the land and enjoy great peace," and your "inheritance will endure forever" (vs. 4, 11, 18). Our Father knows what we need, and he gives us a calling beyond what our lips know what to ask for and beyond what our minds can think up, "more than we could ever ask or imagine" (Ephesians 3:20). It is a call to faith, with hope and certainty, "sure of what we hope for and certain of what we do not see" (Hebrews 11:1, NIV). He gives you a purpose worth investing your time in, a provision that only he can provide and that cannot be bought, and the pursuit of an inheritance that will last well beyond your years here.

> If the Lord delights in a man's way, he makes his steps firm though he stumbles, he will not fall, for the Lord upholds him with his hand. I was young and now I am old, yet I have never seen the righteous forsaken or their children begging bread. They are always generous and lend freely; their children will be blessed.
>
> Psalm 37:23–26 (NIV)

I was caught off guard when I read these verses. In the NLT, verse 23 states that "The steps of the godly are directed by the Lord." How amazing to know that God cares about every detail of our lives. Every man wants the Lord to delight in him, "to take great delight in [him] and rejoice over [him] with singing" (Zephaniah 3:17, NIV). I've spent a lot of time trying to create a secure path and make my steps firm. I thought and if I worked at it hard enough, I wouldn't have to bother God with this stumbling and falling bit.

And as hard as I tried to look past this passage and move ahead, a sledgehammer nailed me between the eyes when I read, "I was young and now I am old…"

Life is so short. Our days on this earth are numbered. What a tragedy it would be to get to the end of our lives and realize that we had really missed out on living, missed our purpose, the provision God has made for us, the inheritance he has in mind for us. How much time do we spend so consumed with securing our own path that we do not see how far we have strayed from the path? And what disasters lie in the wake of that path we have laid? How have we neglected our hearts by pouring all our energy into *our own* desires? How have we neglected God's heart...the heart of our wives...our kids? When all we have laid becomes nothing, how do we start over with God?

> I denied myself nothing my eyes desired; I refused my heart no pleasure. My heart took delight in all my work, and this was the reward for all my labor. Yet when I surveyed all that my hands had done and what I had toiled to achieve, everything was meaningless, a chasing after the wind; nothing was gained under the sun.
>
> Ecclesiastes 2:10–11 (NIV)

## What Inheritance Is Worth Toiling For?

Psalm 1:3 talks about the man who delights in the law of the Lord. It says, "He is like a tree planted by streams of water, which yields its fruit in season and whose leaf does not wither" (Psalm 1:3, NIV).

Trees are a great thing to ponder. Back in the 1950s, my wife's grandfather had purchased a farm just outside Wichita, Kansas. After purchasing the land, they built a little pool house for weekend getaways from the city. During those early years, they also took the time to plant several Pin Oak trees. Roll the clock forward fifty years and now there is a lane of enormous Oak trees, most well over sixty feet tall.

Those trees were there before I was ever born, and when I die, those trees will still probably be there for the next generation to enjoy. Sure there has been pruning and care over the years to keep them healthy, and today, they stand mighty and strong.

Have you started planting some trees in your life? Pruning some branches here and there, refreshing yourself in the rain of God's goodness, deepening your roots into the fertile soil of his Word? What starts as an acorn can stand mighty and tall, enduring the seasons, visible to God above and to children looking up into its branches, an inheritance of eternal proportions.

> Do not store up for yourselves treasures on earth, where moth and rust destroy, and where thieves break in and steal. But store up for yourselves treasures in heaven, where moth and rust do not destroy, and where thieves do not break in and steal. For where your treasure is, there your heart will be also.
>
> Matthew 6:19–21 (NIV)

God has been with you every step along the way, beating in your heart of hearts, following his master design, waiting for you to choose the path he intended for you, giving you life anew.

## Verses to Ponder

My son, give me your heart and let your eyes keep
to my ways.

Proverbs 23:26 (NIV)

As water reflects a face, so a man's heart reflects a
man.

Proverbs 27:19 (NIV)

As iron sharpens iron, so one man sharpens another.

Proverbs 27:17 (NIV)

The Spirit of the Sovereign Lord is on me, because
the Lord has anointed me to preach good news to
the poor. He has sent me to bind up the brokenhearted, to proclaim freedom for the captives and
release from darkness for the prisoners, to proclaim the year of the Lord's favor and the day of
vengeance of our God, to comfort all who mourn,
and provide for those who grieve in Zion—to bestow on them a crown of beauty instead of ashes,
the oil of gladness instead of mourning, and a gar-
ment of praise instead of a spirit of despair.

They will be called oaks of righteousness, a
planting of the Lord for the display of his splendor.

Isaiah 61:1–3 (NIV)

He is like a tree planted by streams of water, which
yields its fruit in season and whose leaf does not
wither. Whatever he does prospers.

Psalm 1:3 (NIV)

## Pulse Check

1) Take a moment to survey your heart. Are there portions of your heart that do not feel alive? Can you identify why? Allow God to penetrate your heart as He speaks to you about those areas and present it to Him as an offering.

2) In what realm do you strive and strain to the point of exhaustion? What would your life be like without that stress and strain? Ask God what He wants to do in the fine details of your heart right now. Does some pruning need to take place?

3) In what recent experience have you felt most alive? How did God bring refreshing in the midst of that experience?

4) Read Isaiah 61:1–3 and Psalm 1:3. Is it difficult to see yourself as an "Oak of Righteousness planted by streams of living water?" Reread Isaiah 61:1–3 out loud, knowing that Jesus is reading this directly to you right now. What emotion does that stir within your heart?

# PLAQUE
## The Plague of Our Hearts

Today we need to draw some blood. If we are going to get serious about getting our hearts right, we've got to allow the Great Physician to get a bit more invasive. Several of you froze up when I mentioned we would be drawing blood—you have some issues with needles and such. So why is it so vital?

The smallest of things can bring the human heart to a halt. Plaque (a combination of gelatinous cholesterol with platelets and fibrin) blocks the blood supply to the arteries providing nutrient and oxygen laden blood to the muscle of the heart. The result can be devastating and life threatening. What we do not recognize is that the danger is there every day. Years of plaque build up, and when it loosens, disaster strikes. It plagues our ability to function as we were intended. The consequences limit us in all spheres of life whether physically, mentally, emotionally, or spiritually.

## The Hidden Plague

The plague of the heart is seen all throughout the Bible. We have read the stories of many who have made bad choices or lost heart. Usually, as we are reading, we can see the disaster as it begins to take shape. We recognize the effects of it upon the generations that follow. From a personal standpoint, though, most of the time those involved in the story had no idea what was brewing and only learned about the issue after the damage had been done. What took place may have been hidden for a time, but eventually the truth came to light.

The truth was never hidden from God. This plague does not catch him by surprise. He knows that he created man for relationship with him, but he also gave man free will. His desire for us and for that relationship with us bridges the gap that sin has created. But to bridge that gap, God takes drastic measures. Enter Jesus.

Prior to his time on the earth, he was God. During his time on the earth, he was *God who became man*—the fruit of the Father to pay for the guilt of our sin. And he laid down his life, shedding his blood so that we could expose what was hidden, come clean, and become whole in our heart. Maybe you have hidden sin or deep, old wounds. Maybe you have bitterness or unforgiveness. Maybe you have pride or rebellion toward God or anger with God. Whatever it may be, Jesus wants to help you remove it and open your heart to him so that you can realize your full potential and live life with vitality. I recognize that it is not easy to recall the day your heart stopped. You remember the day, but you do not want to go there. Pain is never easy to endure, and reentering a place of pain can be emotionally, physically, and mentally disturbing. But our wounds need healing. Our sin needs atonement. Our life needs renewal. Our soul needs a Savior.

## The Numbness of Sudden Death

What events created this mess? Maybe someone very special to us let us down or failed us. Those we thought we could trust hurt us deeply. The wounds remain open, raw, and painful. They will not heal on their own. Only our Surgeon can mend the wounds and bring life back to a place that was dying.

Whether you have suffered some major event that has deeply wounded you, or whether there has been a series of events over your lifetime that has hardened your heart to the things of God, you need to find healing. In the midst of these events, we lose heart. The pain causes us to withdraw from God, from our spouses and our kids—from those who love us the most. We no longer live from our heart. The pain is too great to bear. We have chosen a cold, callused life, because it is safe, and no one can invade the walls that we have surrounded our hearts with. We are locked up securely in a prison of our own making. Somewhere along the way, we quit living, quit being who God made us to be.

## Huck's Heart and Life

On February 18, 2005, a special little boy arrived into our world earlier than expected. We were not prepared for his arrival—he was not due until March thirtieth. Yet he

arrived none the less, all three pounds and eight ounces of
him. Huck Elijah had decided it was time to come out and
join his sister and brothers in the party of the Williamses.
This pregnancy had been a harder pregnancy for my wife,
Shauna. Around twenty weeks, she had some unexplained
bleeding and was on bed rest for three weeks. From that
point on, there was no further bleeding, but she would
still have occasional pains. The day before Huck was born,
I got a call at work from Shauna around noontime. She
thought maybe her water had broken but was just past
thirty-four weeks along in the pregnancy. She was right.
Later that day, we were all headed to Wichita, Shauna by
ambulance and the kids with me. Huck was to be born
very early in the morning on the eighteenth.

Just a couple days after his arrival in the NICU, the
doctor caring for Huck noticed a heart murmur. An echo-
cardiogram later discovered several holes between the
chambers of his heart and also a very narrow area in his
aorta called coarctation of the aorta. Huck was flown from
Wichita to Kansas City where we met with heart special-
ists to try and understand what the next step would be. We
were told he needed to have surgery to correct the coarctation. We were told it should be a pretty straightforward
surgery, but it had not been done on anyone quite so small.

Surgery was rough. Huck's aorta was paper thin and
bled easily as they tried to repair it. They had trouble
keeping his blood pressure up in the range it needed to
be. At the end of surgery, the surgeon shared the news and
discussed the real possibility of Huck needing a second
surgery later that day if improvement was not seen. Not

fifteen minutes after sharing this, he returned and said the second surgery must be done.

We prayed for Huck's life. What more could we pray? What more could we ask? Our world was spinning out of our control. What words could we even come up with to ask? "O God, please..." By the grace of God, Huck survived the second surgery. We hoped for the best, even knowing how difficult it must have been for him during those two surgeries. We were later to find out that his kidneys would no longer work, he had suffered a major stroke, and he was having seizures. We prayed for another miracle, but the one we prayed for did not happen. The wound on his chest from his heart surgery never could be closed completely. His kidneys were never able to make urine. On March 16, 2005, just twenty-six days after his arrival, Huck passed away and went home to be with Jesus.

In the year that passed after his death, I felt empty, abandoned by God, angry, sad, helpless, deeply wounded, and struck with pain I had never before experienced. I felt distant from God. There was a sense of guilt for not praying harder or not having had deep enough faith to believe for healing. I am a physician, and *there was nothing I could do to save Huck*. The memories lingered. My heart suffered. But Jesus was faithful. He never walked away. I was not always welcoming when Jesus came knocking, but I realized, eventually, that only He could bring healing to the place I needed it. Only he was enough to restore my heart.

## The Surgeon and the Knife

Nothing is hidden from God. He knows where we have been, what we have seen and endured, and the deepest pains of our heart. But he is a gentleman. He stands at the door and knocks. "Here I am! I stand at the door and knock. If anyone hears my voice and opens the door, I will come in and eat with him, and he with me" (Revelations 3:20, NIV).

How long has it been since you had a meal with Jesus? Have you ever really tried to think about what that would be like? Jesus shows up at your door, you hear his voice, open the door, and he comes in to hang out with you. He knocks because he loves you and wants more than anything to be invited in. He doesn't want to be left out of our lives. How does he announce his arrival?

*"Here I am! Look, I'm right here at the door of your heart. You don't have to get your heart cleaned up before you ask me in. I know all about the human heart—I made it! That is where I want to be. I want to hang out there, to be with you every step along the way, and to tell you that you've got what it takes. I like what I see in you! Together we are unbeatable, unstoppable, inseparable, one. But you are bleeding—the wound in your heart is festering. You need a skilled surgeon's hand to reach deep into the recesses of your heart and close those wounds for good. I am your Surgeon. I am your Savior."*

Just before Jesus speaks this bit about knocking at the door of your heart, he asks you to do two things. First he says, be earnest. He really wants your heart, but he also wants you to be ready, to be truthful, and to search the depths of your heart.

> O God, you are my God, earnestly I seek you; my
> soul thirsts for you, my body longs for you, in a dry
> and weary land where there is no water.
>
> Psalm 63:1 (NIV)

Secondly, he asks us to repent—bow our knees, open up our hearts, and turn to him. Place your focus on Jesus, not on trying to turn from your sin. Once we get our hearts right, we are pointed back in the right direction by the Holy Spirit. In fact, the Holy Spirit is at work drawing us back to God even before we choose to repent.

> In the same way, the Spirit helps us in our weak-
> ness. We do not know what we ought to pray for,
> but the Spirit himself intercedes for us with groans
> that words cannot express.
>
> Romans 8:26 (NIV)

The Holy Spirit is continually drawing us back into communion with God, allowing us to abide in him, and walk with him. My guess is that if you are reading this, he is working right now to draw you closer to him. Communion, however, is a two-way street. We must *choose* to put ourselves in a place where we can hear from God, commune with him, and abide in him. We cannot afford to put off our relationship with Christ. We cannot afford to leave the door open for Satan to have a foothold.

## Signs of the Times

Unfortunately, many of us don't even bother going to the doctor until maybe we start to see some signs that things are not quite right. Maybe some chest pains here or there, maybe we just can't seem to catch our breath, or maybe it feels like there's an elephant sitting on our chest—not a good sign! We do the exact same thing with Jesus. The pressures in life build. We make some mistakes. We man up and try to fix things the best way we know how. We make more mistakes. That twinge of pain in our chest is starting to get to us. We've harbored bitterness and unforgiveness. We've suffered loss. We've locked our hearts down, lost all emotion, and maybe even turned to some really dark things to help us get by on our own. We think, *Jesus just wouldn't understand my situation. He cannot relate to my pain. I'm so ashamed. No matter what I try, I just cannot seem to get it right. God seems so far away right now.*

But God is very near and he does know our pain. As our Surgeon General, he stands at the ready to revive our hearts, bypass the plaque and restore our hearts to a whole new degree of power and function. Are you ready to go under the knife?

> Today, if you hear his voice, do not harden your hearts . . . For the word of God is living and active. Sharper than any double-edged sword, it penetrates even to dividing soul and spirit, joints and marrow; it judges the thoughts and attitudes of the heart. Nothing in all creation is hidden from God's sight . . . For we do not have a high priest

(Jesus) who is unable to sympathize with our weaknesses, but we have one who has been tempted in every way, just as we are—yet was without sin. Let us then approach the throne of grace with confidence, so that we may receive mercy and find grace to help us in our time of need.

Hebrews 4:7, 12–13, 15–16 (NIV)

Jesus does understand. He has been there in the midst of temptation. He has suffered pain and rejection on our behalf. He laid down his life for us and calls to us: "Come to me, all you who are weary and burdened, and I will give you rest" (Matthew 11:28, NIV). We are told that "if we confess our sins, he is faithful and just and will forgive us our sins and purify us from all unrighteousness" (1 John 1:9, NIV).

He was despised and rejected by men, a man of sorrows, and familiar with suffering. Like one from whom men hide their faces he was despised, and we esteemed him not. Surely he took up our infirmities and carried our sorrows, yet we considered him stricken by God, smitten by him, and afflicted. But he was pierced for our transgressions, he was crushed for our iniquities; the punishment that brought us peace was upon him, and by his wounds we are healed.

Isaiah 53:3–5 (NIV)

Jesus has already done the work at the cross, once and for all. There is no one beyond his reach. The only question is, will you come to him? Will you lay down your pride and bend a knee to admit you cannot do it alone? Will you allow him to enter your heart, enter that deep pain, and walk with you in healing those hidden places? Proverbs 14:10 (NIV) says, "Each heart knows its own bitterness, and no one else can share its joy." New life awaits. Are you willing to step into it?

## How Is Our Heart Able to Heal and Recover?

Anyone who has been through open-heart surgery will tell you that the recovery is rather painful. Coughing and sneezing become unbearably painful; when either of these occurs, it shoots pain throughout your chest and blasts against the sutures and wires that are keeping your chest held together. But with a successful by-pass and recovery, they will also tell you that they feel better than they have in years—in essence, they are alive again.

They made a choice to step out of the weariness of their heart's condition, endure the pain of surgery, and find life. Jesus says, "Come to me, all you who are weary and burdened, and I will give you rest. Take my yoke upon you and learn from me, for I am gentle and humble in heart, and you will find rest for your souls. For my yoke is easy and my burden is light" (Matthew 11:28–30, NIV).

Care to know what is on the other side of the table of life? Take these promises to heart. "I will rejoice over Jerusalem and take delight in my people; the sound of weeping and of crying will be heard in it no more. Before they call I will answer; while they are still speaking I will hear" (Isaiah 65:19, 24, NIV). In Luke chapter 15, Jesus shares with us the story of the prodigal son. Jesus uses this parable to take us to a new depth of understanding of just how our Father wants to welcome you and I home again.

> But while he was still a long way off, his father saw him and was filled with compassion for him; he ran to his son, threw his arms around him and kissed him. The son said to him, "Father, I have sinned against heaven and against you. I am no longer worthy to be called your son." But the father said to his servants, "Quick! Bring the best robe and put it on him. Put a ring on his finger and sandals on his feet. Bring the fattened calf and kill it. Let's have a feast and celebrate. For this son on mine was dead and is alive again; he was lost and is found."
>
> Luke 15:20–23 (NIV)

Take some time right now before you go any further. Ask God to search your heart and speak to those areas that are keeping you from Him. Allow Him to take you into the pain of those old wounds and to stand there with you. Ask the One who has the keys to your heart to unlock the doors, one by one. You can trust him. He knows the pain. "Cast your anxiety upon him because he cares for you" (1 Peter 5:7, NIV). There is no shame, only forgiveness. As an act of complete trust and obedience, offer your heart to Jesus.

You may need to linger there for a while, and listen to what Jesus has to share with you. Some of the areas may need an added measure of diligence and prayer to give over and you may need to seek out the trusted prayers of a brother in Christ. Write down what you see and what Jesus speaks to you. Mark this day on your calendar.

> On the last and greatest day of the Feast, Jesus
> stood and said in a loud voice, "If anyone is thirsty,
> let him come to me and drink. Whoever believes
> in me, as the Scripture has said, streams of living
> water will flow from within him."
>
> John 7:37–38 (NIV)

I shared part of the story about Huck earlier in this chapter, but the story did not end there. On March 30, 2005, Huck's original due date, our oldest daughter Rachael gave her heart to Jesus. On February 19, 2006, exactly one year and one day after Huck was born, we welcomed Zebediah Chance into our family. God was faithfully mending our wounds. And in 2008, we adopted two children, Jennifer Carolina and Gabriel Alejandro, from Nicaragua. Gabe was born in the same month Huck was born. Tell me God is not into details! It was as if God closed the chapter on suffering and started a new chapter in our lives—a chapter filled with joy.

I am thankful and grateful for the lessons God taught us through Huck's life and the days that followed. We were touched by the outpouring of family and friends in that time and how Huck touched the lives of so many who prayed for him. Yet I know God's providence is in the details. Had Huck lived, he would have been a special child with special needs. It is hard to say whether we would have chosen to have more kids. With ongoing medical expenses, adoption would probably never have happened for us. With the death of one child, many others were affected. With the death of God's Son, our hearts and eternity are forever changed.

## Verses to Ponder

> But whatever was to my profit I now consider loss for the sake of Christ. What is more, I consider everything a loss compared to the surpassing greatness of knowing Christ Jesus my Lord, for whose sake I have lost all things.
>
> I consider them rubbish, that I may gain Christ and be found in him, not having a righteousness of my own that comes from the law, but that which is through faith in Christ—the righteousness that comes from God and is by faith. I want to know Christ and the power of his resurrection and the fellowship of sharing in his sufferings, becoming like him in his death, and so, somehow, to attain to the resurrection from the dead…I press on to take hold of that for which Christ Jesus took hold of me.
>
> Philippians 3:7–12 (NIV)

## Pulse Check

1) Is there a moment in life you can recall when your heart stopped from wounds you suffered? Is that heart ache still there? If it is, will you allow Jesus to walk with you into that wound and heal you?

2) Is there a root of bitterness or unforgiveness attached to the pain in your heart? Are you willing to give that over to Jesus and be released from that right now?

3) Ask the Holy Spirit to give you a picture of how He sees your heart. Is He asking anything more from you as you seek Him?

4) Scars may remain, but the wounds no longer need to remain bleeding, bare, and open. Write this time down. Make your scars a story to share with others—a story that reveals the true nature of our Savior and Surgeon.

# DIET

## Tales of the Table

Everyone has heard the phrase, "You are what you eat." So could it be true? It seems like everywhere we look, there are commercials about tasty food in great restaurants, all you can eat salad bars, and other wonderful meals that are just ready to throw in the oven and cook at home. If you wait a commercial or two, the very next thing you see is an ad for Weight Watchers or Slim-Fast or more drastic measures such as surgery to take the weight off. So where is the happy medium? Do we consume all that we see, or do we starve ourselves to the point of wilting away? Where is the balance?

I'm sure issues concerning diet and weight have been brought up by you or by your doctor. Food, after all, provides us with the sustenance we need to perform daily functions, to have energy to survive, and to provide the building blocks we need to stay healthy and grow. In excess however, we can see the effects on the scales and in our waistline. We can also see the ill effects of eating too little with anorexia and bulimia. Having a healthy perspective of food is vital to our life and health. The Bible gives a spiritual perspective on the importance of food. Time and again we find that what we consume with our minds has an impact on our spiritual vitality, life, and growth.

We do not have to look too far into Genesis to see that an unhealthy food choice can have eternal implications. God told Adam and Eve that they could have all the plants in the Garden of Eden for food as well as the fruit from the trees in the garden. There was one tree in the middle of the garden, however, that they were not to eat from. We know about Eve being deceived by the serpent, Adam doing nothing to stop the serpent's influence or Eve from taking the fruit, and the sudden fall of man.

And what about Esau and Jacob? For a bowl of stew, Esau sold his birthright. Later, Jacob and Rebekah deceptively tricked Isaac into giving the blessing of the firstborn to Jacob.

After Moses leads the Israelites out of Egypt, God uses quail and manna to feed them as they wander in the desert. Despite God being adamant about his instructions for collecting the food, the Israelites still struggle to get it right. Some of the Israelites tried to keep enough manna to last for tomorrow and it rots. Others paid no attention to resting on the Sabbath, and they went out to search for manna and find none. God is setting up the idea that he wants to be our *daily provision,* that we would come to him to receive our *daily bread.*

## The Bread of Life

Jesus calls himself the *Bread of Life* in John 6. As we read further in that chapter, Jesus compares his body to bread and his blood to wine and asks that we partake in the feast he has prepared for us.

> I tell you the truth, unless you eat the flesh of the Son of Man and drink his blood, you have no life in you.
>
> John 6:53 (NIV)

What is the significance of Jesus asking us to *feed on him?* He tells us that if we do that "we remain in him and he in us" and "he who feeds on this bread will live forever" (John 6:56, 58, NIV). Even after Jesus was resurrected, he used food to speak to his disciples. Recall in John 21 that Jesus had not yet appeared to the disciples after the resurrection, namely Simon Peter and Thomas. And what was it that they decided to do just days after their friend and Savior was slain upon the cross? They went back to their old jobs as fishermen.

> So they went out and got into the boat, but that night they caught nothing. Early in the morning, Jesus stood on the shore, but the disciples did not realize it was Jesus. "Friends, haven't you any fish?"
>
> "No," they answered.
>
> So Jesus tells them to "Throw your net on the right side of the boat and you will find some."
>
> John 21:3–6 (NIV)

Jesus had to get a chuckle out of this event, even in resur-rected form. As I read these verses, I could almost hear him laughing while these *serious fishermen* were at work. Who is to say that they were not having trouble getting tangled in their nets, after all it had been over three years since they'd been fishing. I think Jesus might have even disguised his voice when he shouted at them. And was it a common practice for someone to yell from shore and tell them where to cast the nets?

We read on and find that it was such a huge catch that they were unable to haul in the net, eerily similar to a previous scenario. And suddenly, like a lightning strike, Peter recognizes Jesus and jumps into the water, still one hundred yards from the shore! When they all arrived at shore, Jesus has a fire of burning coals with fish on it and some bread. He tells them, "Come and have breakfast" (John 21:12, NIV).

## A Basketful of Miracles

Food. It has significance to God. It has significance to us. And time after time throughout the Bible we see food play an integral role in the teaching and training of the Israelites, in growing the faith of the disciples, and in pro-viding for needs in common with the early church. Look at Jesus's life: his first miracle was turning water into wine, he used a few loaves and fish two different times to feed thousands, and he placed special importance on having the last meal with His disciples.

As evening approached, the disciples came to him and said, "This is a remote place, and it's already getting late. Send the crowds away, so they can go to the villages and buy themselves some food."

Jesus replied, "They do not need to go away. You give them something to eat."

"We have here only five loaves of bread and two fish," they answered.

"Bring them here to me," he said. And he directed the people to sit down on the grass. Taking the five loaves and the two fish and looking up to heaven, he gave thanks and broke the loaves. Then he gave them to the disciples, and the disciples gave them to the people. They all ate and were satisfied, and the disciples picked up twelve basketfuls of broken pieces that were left over. The number of those who ate was about five thousand men, besides women and children.

Matthew 14:15–21 (NIV)

Loaves and fish. Basketfuls of leftovers. *Everyone was satisfied.* And as if the point were not already obvious, Jesus does it again in Chapter 15 of Matthew. Jehovah Jireh, God our provider. What was Jesus trying to teach the disciples then and what is he trying to teach us as his disciples now?

It is more than just getting our stomachs full and pressing on for another day. Jesus shows us that he can do much with a little—feed thousands with a few fish and loaves, make himself known to the world through twelve friends, and change our circumstances and our perspective with just a little faith. The question for today is, *are we hungry for the things of God?* Or are we simply satisfied with something other than the provision God has for us today?

> Meanwhile his disciples urged him, "Rabbi, eat something."
> But he said to them, "I have food to eat that you know nothing about."
> Then his disciples said to each other, "Could someone have brought him food?"
> "My food," said Jesus, "is to do the will of him who sent me and to finish his work."
>
> John 4:31–34 (NIV)

## Satisfaction and Deception

Whether we realize it or admit it, our souls hunger and thirst for the things of God, for real food that satisfies our every longing and quenches our deepest thirst. Unfortunately, we are also easily deceived, just like Eve and Esau, into believing that we know what our bodies need. We choose to feed ourselves on things that seem *good*, but maybe are not always the *best*—and good may very well be the enemy of best. Or we blatantly choose to disregard God's diet and chew on things that bring us momentary satisfaction but usually with a bitter aftertaste.

Unfortunately our eyes have been allured by the patterns of this world and they deceive us at times. The eyes are able to trick our minds into believing something other than the truth. This is called deception. Just think back to last Thanksgiving. Remember your plate—all that turkey, and stuffing, and cranberry salad, and gravy, and pecan pie? Remember how you felt when you finished off your plate (maybe for the second or third time even)? A little bit of this and a little bit of that became a little bit too much. Though our plates were full, it did not really satisfy. What we find in the end is that we have a huge gut ache, and we leave our hearts starving for things that truly bring us life. The enemy's deception is no different today than it was at the time of the Garden of Eden. He wants us to settle for a counterfeit rather than truly find the food that satisfies our souls.

What am I talking about? Satan is the author of counterfeits, things that deceive us just enough to make it seem like we are satisfied. Little by little, these things start to take the place of God in our lives. We give up spending time in his Word, communing with him in prayer, giving ourselves time to worship him, or gathering together to celebrate what he is doing in our lives. We do not mean to do this, it's just that circumstances prevail and we tend to squeeze God out of the picture.

I'm not saying any of the following are curses of Satan, all I'm saying is that we need to pay attention to our bodies and to our hearts and know what we are feeding on. Here are a few examples. Late nights at work keep us from getting up early to meet with God, but we know he will understand. Things get busy at church with our ministry needs and between all the doing for God to make the ministry happen, we lose track of our hearts in good works. We miss what God is trying to do *in* us. The kids have a soccer game today right in the middle of time for church, but we want them to know they are important to us. We choose to skip church for the sake of running all over the city for another game.

And what about our time at home? We always seem to run out of quality time with our family. Our minds are strung out from a day's worth of work that we cannot seem to leave at the office. We just want to check out in front of our favorite program. The big game is on tonight and we just can't miss it! What about when the kids all go to bed and we are alone with our TV? What channels do we flip to then? What do our desires turn to? What do we get *hungry* for? We tell ourselves that one little look is all we will take, or we will turn the channel when those scenes are shown. The list goes on and on, and over time our hearts slowly and steadily waste away without God's input in our lives. Where there used to be clarity, now there resides a thick fog and our view of God become limited. Luckily we have the writer of Hebrews and Paul's letters that encourage us back to our source of life.

> Therefore, since we are surrounded by such a great cloud of witnesses, let us throw off everything that hinders and the sin that so easily entangles, and let us run with perseverance the race marked out for us. Let us fix our eyes on Jesus, the author and perfecter of our faith, who for the joy set before him endured the cross, scorning its shame, and sat down at the right hand of the throne of God.
>
> Hebrews 12:1–2 (NIV)

We need to trade in our fog of deception for the great cloud of witnesses. We each have a race that has been marked out for us, but we cannot race without an energy source. We need the Bread of Life. The race *requires* perseverance. We must also be focused—fix our eyes on the prize.

## The Secret of Contentment

We need to have the attitude of Paul, who despite knowing firsthand the suffering and persecution of following Christ, still exhibited a life which helped to transform and grow the New Testament churches to which he wrote. He shares his life intimately with us throughout the New Testament epistles.

> I know what it is to be in need, and I know what it is to have plenty. I have learned the secret of being content in any and every situation, whether well fed or hungry, whether living in plenty or in want. I can do everything through him who gives me strength.
>
> Philippians 4:12–13 (NIV)

Are you trusting Jesus for that secret of contentment? Have you tasted the Bread of Life and found your true strength? He invites you to a feast each and every day…"*Come and have breakfast.*" Renew your strength in him and feed upon his Word.

## Verses to Ponder

> Don't copy the behavior and customs of this world, but let God transform you into a new person by changing the way you think. Then you will know

what God wants you to do, and you will know how good and pleasing and perfect his will really is.

Romans 12:2 (NLT)

My son, if you accept my words and store up my commands within you, turning your ear to wisdom and applying you heart to understanding, and if you call out for insight and cry aloud for understanding, and if you look for it as for silver and search for it as for hidden treasure, then you will understand the fear of the Lord and find the knowledge of God.

Proverbs 2:1–5 (NIV)

Then you will understand what is right and just and fair—every good path. For wisdom will enter your heart, and knowledge will be pleasant to your soul. Discretion will protect you, and understanding will guard you.

Proverbs 2:9–11 (NIV)

Your word is a lamp unto my feet and a light unto my path.

Psalm 199:105 (NIV)

Follow my advice, my son; always treasure my commands. Obey them and live! Guard my teachings as your most precious possession. Tie them on your fingers as a reminder. Write them deep within your heart.

Proverbs 7:1–3 (NLT)

## Pulse Check

1) What is the last food commercial that you remember? Did what your eyes see make you believe that was just what you needed? What is the truth about what you saw? Did you ever consider that your eyes might have deceived you into believing that more food is just what you needed?

2) What unhealthy habits of eating does this study bring to mind? What healthy habits do you presently follow? What does *Daily Bread* mean to you?

3) Are you presently satisfied? Do you hunger more for the things of God? Have you encountered any counterfeits that left you with a gut ache? How would you define contentment?

4) How have choices at the table over the years affected your physical body and physical health? How have choices and priorities affected your time with God? How does this show up in your spiritual life? Have you ever thought of fasting from food to remind yourself of your need for Daily Bread?

# REGULAR EXERCISE

## Running the Race

Have you ever been in training for a race, maybe a 10K, half marathon, or a full marathon? If you have or if you know someone who has, you know that you just don't sign up for the race the day before and decide to run it. More than likely, training began many weeks earlier and required a rather rigorous schedule to prepare for the race. Taking time to review various resources on training schedules, stretching exercises, managing eating habits, and mentally preparing for the race were prerequisites. Training required a time commitment of at least four or five days per week and various sacrifices to be able to reach the target race date.

From a medical perspective, regular physical exercise has several lasting qualities that endure beyond the end of any race. Regular exercise can improve muscle tone, which impacts metabolism and contributes to a leaner body mass. It helps reduce stress, enhance sleep, boost your immune system, and improve your mood. Moderate physical activity can also improve aerobic capacity of the heart and protect against cardiovascular disease, diabetes, and obesity. These are just a few of the reasons doctors are always encouraging patients to devote time to physical activity.

Why is it so difficult to maintain a level of fitness for the average person? Most everyone would love to have the benefits of physical activity and have all the positive cardiovascular effects that come with it. Why is it so difficult to count the cost, take the time, stick with those New Year's resolutions, and get out of bed in the morning? People are willing to spend the money to buy the newest and latest equipment to encourage them to get with it or to buy their yearly membership at the fitness club. But buying the equipment or the membership does not guarantee success, especially if there is no desire or discipline to use them. The prize does not always go to the fastest (or the one with the most money), but to the one that endures, perseveres, and has trained long and hard enough to finish.

## Overcoming the Weekend Warrior

Several years ago I began training for a half marathon. I was never much of a long distance runner, but after my son passed away, I poured myself into running. It became an outlet for me to burn off frustration and pain, a time alone with God to try to make sense of all our family had just been through and to try to find solace for my soul. It became a healthy resource to unload my mind and focus my attention. Physical pain became a distraction from the anguish of my heart, and I committed myself to a directed course of training every week, running four or five days a week and covering upwards of twenty to twenty-five miles per week. With time, the pounds came off as the miles increased, and I closely watched what I ate. I developed muscle in my legs that I had never noticed before, and my endurance improved every week of training. In June of that year, I ran my first half marathon. It felt good to set a goal and reach it.

Despite all that training four years ago, I would not even begin to consider running that race this year. Why? Because I have not been training. Without having run consistently over the last several months, it would be a major struggle to get through that race. So can we apply this to spiritual principles also? We, as men, are known all too well for our weekend warrior mentality. We give no thought or consideration to preparing ourselves during the week for what we plan to do on the weekend. So when Saturday shows up, we think we are ready for anything you can throw at us. Need some helping building that garage? Sure, no problem. Want to play a pickup game of basketball? I can do that. Are you available to help some friends move their piano? You bet.

Of course, Sunday always follows Saturday, and a day or two or three after brutalizing our bodies, we find that we are a little achy and sore. Our body reminds us we are not the teenagers we used to be. The problem is that we cannot do that with our walk with God. If we have not taken time to build spiritual muscle, there is nothing to fall back on when we need to be strong in our faith. It requires training, time in the Word daily, personal times of prayer and worship, and times of solitude. We cannot get all we need from God one day a week, namely on Sunday morning. "Whatever you have learned or received or heard from me, or seen in me—put it into practice. And the God of peace will be with you" (Philippians 4:9, NIV).

Have we seen Christ displayed before us in the lives of others? Has the Word of God been spoken to us or preached to us recently? Are we surrounding ourselves with people who can encourage us in our walk, a group of guys or a mentor to help us in the fight for our faith? Paul encourages us to *put it into practice.* We need our time with God. God wants to display his glory through us. The world needs to see and hear and feel Christ near them that others can also be brought into the kingdom of God. We are powerless without God's influence in our lives. When the world wages against us to destroy us with all its warped entanglements, wouldn't it be great to remember the God of peace has our back and is fighting on our behalf?

> Do you not know that in a race all the runners run, but only one gets the prize? Run in such a way as to get the prize. Everyone who competes in the games goes into strict training. They do it to get a crown that will not last; but we do it to get a crown that will last forever. Therefore I do not run like a man running aimlessly; I do not fight like a man beating the air. No, I beat my body and make it my slave so that after I have preached to others, I myself will not be disqualified for the prize.
>
> 1 Corinthians 9:24–27 (NIV)

Whether we like it or not, *we are in a race!* And to some degree we are also training our bodies. But for what or for whom are we training? What is our ultimate goal? What is the prize we are seeking—things of God or things of the world? There are only two choices.

## The Shaping of Our Hearts

So how do we exercise our heart spiritually? Here is a rundown of the ways we can get our hearts in shape to hear from God. The first is worship and adoration, whether individually or corporately. Secondly, we need to be spending time before God in prayer to tune our hearts to hear his voice and to fight off the enemy that keeps us from drawing near to God. Thirdly, we need the Word. With it we can hear what God is speaking to us, use passages in worship, meditation and prayer, learn how to keep our minds sharp to defend ourselves and to grow in our walk, and feed our hungry souls with its nourishment. These are skills *basic* to our survival and our hearts need the exercise with God daily, *not just on weekends.* There is no magical formula to any of the elements above. However, there is one basic element that if missing will kill any hope of getting on God's treadmill: *time.*

Without taking time to pray, it will never happen. Without setting aside time for worship, the heart will never sing. Without planning for time in the Word, the soul will starve. What we will find is that when we take the time, God rewards our efforts. And over time, as we begin to develop and tailor our walk with God in worship, prayer, and study of his Word, we might find ourselves surprised by the pounding of our hearts. *Strength, endurance, perseverance, character, hope.*

> Therefore, since we have been justified through faith, we have peace with God through our Lord Jesus Christ, through whom we have gained access by faith into this grace in which we now stand. And we rejoice in the hope of the glory of God. Not only so, but we also rejoice in our sufferings, because we know that suffering produces perseverance; perseverance, character; and character, hope. And hope does not disappoint us, because God has poured out his love into our hearts by the Holy Spirit, whom he has given us.
>
> Romans 5:1–5 (NIV)

If we have exercised at all, we know that it is a form of suffering. Exercise also requires a great sacrifice of time. Sure there are a million things we want to get done today, but there is only one thing that we really need—time with God. It will require sacrifice, and it may seem like suffering when we are forced to choose God over some of those things that we look at as being important. But when we really find God, when we press into prayer and worship and his Word, what we thought was important fades away. We find *life* as we sit at his table and dine on the *Bread of Life*. And suddenly, we find ourselves delighting in our sacrifice and our suffering as we exercise our hearts. And all the while, God is right there with us. He is the master trainer, and his Word has laid out an amazing exercise plan for our hearts.

## Walking in Worship

> Then God said, "Take your son, your only son,
> Isaac, whom you love, and go to the region of
> Moriah. Sacrifice him there as a burnt offering on
> one of the mountains I will tell you about." Early
> the next morning Abraham got up and saddled his
> donkey. He took with him two of his servants and
> his son Isaac. When he had cut enough wood for
> the burnt offering, he set out for the place God
> had told him about. On the third day Abraham
> looked up and saw the place in the distance. He
> said to his servants, "Stay here with the donkey
> while I and the boy go over there. We will worship
> and then we will come back to you."
>
> Genesis 22:2–5 (NIV)

Abraham knew about sacrifice and suffering when it came to
worship. He was prepared to turn God's promise of his family lineage into a burnt offering. Yet God spared Isaac and
rewarded Abraham for his obedience. He had made a habit
of spending time with God in worship, and he knew God's
heart. There is no mention here of Abraham ever ques-
tioning God about his motives or his goal in this process.
Abraham did not know there were alternate plans until the
ram showed up in the thicket. Yet he chose to go worship out
of obedience to God and out of reverence and fear of God,
knowing that God's ultimate plan would succeed.

"Do not worship any other god, for the Lord, whose
name is Jealous, is a jealous God" (Exodus 34:14, NIV). In
this verse in Exodus, we learn more about the God we
serve. He is jealous for our attention. He knows about all

the distractions in our lives that keep us from him, but can you comprehend how elated he gets when we choose time with him over something else? Can you begin to understand the joy of a father when his son takes time to be with him or give him recognition for just being Dad?

Imagine yourself for a moment watching your son nail the three-pointer to win the state championship or smash a home run with two down in the bottom of the ninth inning with the bases loaded to win the game—grand slam! How awesome it is to see your son celebrating: the crowd roars, the court gets rushed with fans, and the dugout clears. You watch in awe at the accomplishment of your son and know he will remember this forever. But in the midst of the crowded court or as he turns down the third base line, he gives you *the look,* and your eyes meet. In the middle of one of his greatest moments in life, he looks to you to share it with him, and your heart leaps for joy. God's heart leaps for joy every day when we choose to meet with him. He's jumping up and down in the stands screaming, *"That's my boy! That's my boy!"* He is a jealous God.

> "Yet a time is coming and has now come when the true worshipers will worship the Father in spirit and truth, for they are the kind of worshipers the Father seeks. God is Spirit, and his worshipers must worship in spirit and in truth."
>
> John 4:23–24 (NIV)

This passage is taken from Jesus's meeting with the Samaritan woman at the well. He uses this time to speak with her about what is seen versus that which is unseen.

Hebrews 11:1 tells us (NIV), "Faith is being sure of what we hope for and certain of what we do not see." Compare the verses in John 4 above with John 6:63 (NIV), "The Spirit gives life; the flesh counts for nothing. The words I have spoken to you are Spirit and they are life." The radical point of this message is what is seen is only temporary and is not reality. To worship in Spirit and Truth is to believe in the eternal God and to have faith beyond what our physical eyes can see. We need to see with our hearts. If we worship for the sake of performing, for the sake of posing, or for the sake of checking a box, it counts for nothing. God desires to make himself known to us through worship, and we cannot do that in our flesh, only by the Spirit of God that fills our heart.

Interestingly, early on in Jesus's interaction with the Samaritan woman in John 4, he shares with her these words, "Everyone who drinks this water will be thirsty again, but whoever drinks the water I give him will never thirst" (John 4:13–14, NIV). Exercise (*worship*) will make us thirsty.

Paul sums it up very well: "Therefore, I urge you, brothers, in view of God's mercy, to offer your bodies as living sacrifices, holy and pleasing to God–this is your spiritual act of worship" (Romans 12:1, NIV). Offer your time, your heart, and your energy as a living sacrifice. If we're not living sacrifices, then we are probably *dead*. Walk in worship, get your heart in shape, overcome the weekend warrior, and find that your thirst is finally quenched.

## Practicing in Prayer

Jesus taught his disciples to pray and gave us the Lord's Prayer. He prepared for his ministry on the Mount of Olives in prayer, and most of his miracles were performed after days or nights in solitude with God. There are amazing prayers throughout the scriptures that can be read aloud as prayers for us.

> One day Jesus was praying in a certain place. When he finished, one of his disciples said to him, "Lord, teach us to pray, just as John taught his disciples."
>
> He said to them, "When you pray, say: 'Father, hallowed be your name, your kingdom come. Give us each day our daily bread. Forgive us our sins, for we also forgive everyone who sins against us. And lead us not into temptation.' "
>
> Luke 11:2–5 (NIV)

Praise and adoration (hallowed be your name), supplication (daily bread), confession (forgive our sins), and warfare (fighting temptation). Jesus shows us how to exercise our faith through prayer, how to build our prayer muscles. As our personal advisor and trainer, Jesus gives us some pointers on how to sharpen our prayer life. His disciples saw him go off to pray on multiple occasions and were amazed at his insight and authority. Jesus knew how important the exercise of prayer was in keeping his mind, body, and spirit in tune with his Father in heaven. Exercise in prayer. Jesus finished with the following verses:

And so I tell you, keep on asking, and you will be
given what you ask for. Keep on looking, and you
will find. Keep on knocking, and the door will be
opened. For everyone who asks, receives. Everyone
who seeks, finds. And the door is opened to everyone who knocks. If you sinful people know how to
give good gifts to your children, how much more
will your heavenly Father give the Holy Spirit to
those who ask him.

Luke 11:9–10, 13 (NLT)

Jesus sat down with his disciples to teach them how to pray.
Interestingly, they had actually asked him to teach them.
Why? I think we all know that prayer is important, but we
do not always get an image of just how important it is in
God's eyes. Prayer is not so much for asking for things we
want, seeking more of God's blessings, or knocking at the
door of opportunity. Prayer is *learning to abide* with God,
communing with Him, catching a glimpse of how he sees
life and how he sees us fitting into it. It is no wonder the
disciples asked. They had spent time with Jesus and were
intrigued by his devotion to prayer.

Luke chapter 11 starts off with Jesus "praying in a certain place." That makes me curious. What was the certain place? This was not the first time that Jesus had gone
off to a solitary place to pray or to the Mount of Olives.
Prayer is a continual part of Jesus's life. He teaches us
how to abide in constant communion with the Father,
how to feast on our daily bread in prayer, how to be filled
with the water that quenches every thirst. But when
he gets to verse nine, Jesus exhorts his disciples (us) to

"Ask…seek…knock…" (Luke 11:9, NIV). He exhorts us to put our faith in action.

I think many of us have a general idea about what it means to ask and seek, but sometimes we need to knock. We need to really hear from God on some difficult issues. Have you ever been there, pounding at God's door and maybe not because you are really happy? God was there too, and he is there now. Your pounding does not catch him off guard. He has not been sleeping. He has been waiting for you to come rattle his door. What you may not have seen was the door fly open wide as he leapt out to grab you in his arms and hold you close, all the while your hands beating into his chest. He is our loving Father, and he longs to hold us close during those hard times much as we would hold our son or daughter close to our chest when they are injured or upset. Love covers a multitude of sins. You might need to take a moment to spend with Dad. I know I need to.

"But when you pray, go into your room, close the door and pray to your Father, who is unseen. Then your Father, who sees what is done in secret, will reward you" (Matthew 6:6, NIV). Our Father longs to be alone with us, and he knows we need to get away from everything. Turn the TV and the music off, close the door on distractions. You may need a pencil and paper while you are praying. Turn the cell phone off and open your heart to God. Allow the Holy Spirit to penetrate the silence and speak to your heart.

> Immediately Jesus made the disciples get into the boat and go on ahead of him to the other side, while he dismissed the crowd. After he had dismissed

them, he went up on a mountainside by himself to pray. When evening came, he was there alone, but the boat was already a considerable distance from land, buffeted by the waves because the wind was against it. During the fourth watch of the night Jesus went out to them, walking on the lake.

Matthew 14:22–25 (NIV)

We need to get alone with God to understand what he is calling us to do. If Jesus had attempted to walk on water in human strength even, he would have been in over his head, quite literally. Once again he was deliberate in his time alone with his Father, and once again his disciples were amazed when he appeared to them on the lake. We need God's perspective.

"Watch and pray so that you will not fall into temptation. The spirit is willing, but the body is weak" (Matthew 26:41, NIV). Satan does not like it when we pray. So, to keep us from prayer, he likes to take some cheap shots at us when we are weary, tired, stressed, and alone. That's where warfare becomes pivotal. Pray the scriptures out loud and by all means turn your cell phone back on and call a brother to sound the alarm in prayer. *We do not fight alone.* Ephesians 6 also reminds us of the battle we are in and the need to put on the full armor of God. Does any warrior ever go to battle unprepared and come out victorious?

In the same way, the Spirit helps us in our weakness. We do not know what we ought to pray for, but the Spirit himself intercedes for us with groans that words cannot express. And he who searches

> our hearts knows the mind of the Spirit, because the Spirit intercedes for the saints in accordance with God's will.
>
> Romans 8:26–27 (NIV)

The Spirit loves to intercede on our behalf especially when we are speechless. The other wonderful news is that Jesus is at the right hand of God the Father interceding on our behalf day and night. There is no escaping. And should you happen to stumble along the way, he is there to pick you up and dust you off. But he also asks us to let others in on our lives, our successes, and our struggles. We are at war. We battle together. We might get wounded. When that happens, we will need someone to bandage our wounds. We cannot afford to lose heart or to turn from the battle. "Therefore confess your sins to each other and pray for each other so that you may be healed. The prayer of a righteous man is powerful and effective" (James 5:16, NIV).

## Working out with the Word

> In the beginning was the Word, and the Word was with God, and the Word was God. He was with God in the beginning. Through him all things were made; without him nothing was made that has been made. In him was life, and that life was the light of men.
>
> John 1:1–4 (NIV)

John describes Jesus as the Word, the one who was with God in the very beginning. It seems to make sense that we should go to the Word for life and enlightenment, to help us see clearly each and every day.

> But as for you, continue in what you have learned and have become convinced of, because you know those from whom you learned it, and how from infancy you have known the Holy Scriptures, which are able to make you wise for salvation through faith in Christ Jesus. All Scripture is God breathed and is useful for teaching, rebuking, correcting and training in righteousness, so that the man of God may be thoroughly equipped for every good work.
>
> 2 Timothy 3:14–18 (NIV)

Spending time with God's Word is training in righteousness, equipping us for all that we are called to by God. It keeps us on a firm foundation and keeps us in line and heading in the right direction. It is food from God, breathing his life into us.

"Thy word is a lamp unto my feet and a light unto my path" (Psalm 119:105, NIV). Ever been caught out in the dark without a flashlight? It's pretty difficult to see a clear path. Even on moonlit nights, it can be hard to avoid the holes in the path and keep from turning an ankle. But God's Word lights a very clear, brilliant path in this darkened world we live in. Through his Word, God provides a solid path for us to follow him. His light clearly leads us and helps us avoid the pitfalls in life.

> How can a young man keep his way pure? By living according to your word. I seek you with all my

heart; do not let me stray from your commands. I have hidden your word in my heart that I might not sin against you.

Psalm 119:9–11 (NIV)

What is the most recent verse you have put into the storage bank of your heart? The Word is vital for life and vital to define and defend against sin and temptation. Notice in the verse below how Jesus answered Satan when confronted with temptation. He used the Word of God for warfare and to defend against Satan's attack. "Jesus answered, 'It is written: Man does not live on bread alone, but on every word that comes from the mouth of God'" (Matthew 4:4, NIV).

The battle we are in is a battle for the very hearts and lives of people and a battle for the glory of the kingdom of God. "For our battle is not against flesh and blood, but against the rulers and authorities and powers of this dark world and against the spiritual forces of evil in the heavenly realms" (Ephesians 6:12, NLT). As discussed before, we have the armor we need for the battle at hand. And remember the offensive weapon we have in our hand: the sword of the Spirit. "Take the helmet of salvation and the sword of the Spirit, which is the word of God" (Ephesians 6:17, NIV). *If we don't use it, it just becomes another piece of equipment to drag around!* We are not given any other weapon with which to fight. Think of the biceps you will build if you use the sword as it was intended to be used. Biceps have to be strengthened through a process of exercising, training, flexing, and lifting. The simple rule applies: use it or lose it!

We are also called to use the Word to teach others and to encourage other in their walk with Christ. "Let the word of Christ dwell in you richly as you teach and admonish one another with all wisdom, and as you sing psalms, hymns and spiritual songs with gratitude in your hearts to God" (Colossians 3:16, NIV).

Do not think that the Word of God is not powerful or as sharp as a razor. God has spoken his Word to be able to penetrate deep within our souls, to draw us to him, and to convict us of our need for him in our lives. He knows our hearts better than we do, but we can get insight into the heart if we will spend time in his Word. As we exercise our hearts, we learn about the capacity of the treasure that God has hidden deep within our hearts. Each time we exercise, we are stretched, our trust is deepened, and our faith grows. With time, he reveals the deepest longings of our hearts to us.

> For the word of God is living and active. Sharper than any double-edged sword, it penetrates even to dividing soul and spirit, joints and marrow; it judges the thoughts and attitudes of the heart.
>
> Hebrews 4:12 (NIV)

Walking in worship, practicing in prayer, working out in the Word—we've merely scratched the surface as we look into the extreme importance that God places upon spending time with him. He says that out of the overflow of our hearts, our mouth speaks. Out of this overflow of the heart we are able to reach out to others and find relationships that bring God honor. At some point in our lives

God may have called us out of a relationship, because he had something different in mind for us, or he was asking us to leave the past behind. As we mature he calls us to reach out to the lost, to care for orphans and widows, to put ourselves in harm's way for his glory. God cares about people and asks us to have the same compassion as he does. But until we are in a right relationship with him, we will struggle to do right by our fellow man.

Are there some relationships you need to bring to the Father? Do you need to seek forgiveness from a brother or from your wife? Are you looking after those around you the way God intended for you too? Are you getting time to spend with those most important to you? What does your life impart to them? Are you leaving a legacy and an inheritance worth keeping? Exercise of the heart is an exercise of faith. "Faith is being sure of what we hope for and certain of what we do not see" (Hebrews 11:1, NIV). Exercise begets faith and faith begets obedience, obedience to God and to his calling on us to affect lives around us for the glory of his kingdom.

## Verses to Ponder

> For it is we who are the circumcision, we who worship by the Spirit of God, who glory in Christ Jesus, and who put no confidence in the flesh.
> Philippians 3:3 (NIV)

> Therefore, since we are receiving a kingdom that cannot be shaken, let us be thankful, and so worship God acceptably with reverence and awe…
> Hebrews 12:28 (NIV)

Do not be anxious about anything, but in every-thing, by prayer and petition, with thanksgiving, present your requests to God.

Philippians 4:6 (NIV)

Therefore I tell you, whatever you ask for in prayer, believe that you have received it, and it will be yours.

Mark 11:24 (NIV)

Consequently, faith comes from hearing the mes-sage, and the message is heard through the word of Christ.

Romans 10:17 (NIV)

Do your best to present yourself to God as one ap-proved, a workman who does not need to be ashamed and who correctly handles the word of truth.

2 Timothy 2:15 (NIV)

Do you not know? Have you not heard? The Lord is the everlasting God, the Creator of the ends of the earth. He will not grow tired or weary, and his understanding no one can fathom. He gives strength to the weary and increases the power of the weak. Even youths grow tired and weary, and young men stumble and fall; but those who hope in the Lord will renew their strength. They will soar on wings like eagles; they will run and not grow weary, they will walk and not be faint.

Isaiah 40:28–31 (NIV)

## Pulse Check

1) How is the race going at this point? Are you still running? What challenges lie in the way of improving your training skills? Do you recognize a prize worth pursuing? As you continue to pursue God, remember that it is a process without end—the ultimate goal is to know him.

2) Would you agree that exercising includes some degree of suffering, at least initially? Do you recognize other areas in life where you have chosen to suffer for the sake of gaining something of value? What do you think of Jim Elliott's words: *He is no fool who gives what he cannot keep to gain what he cannot lose?*

3) As you consider opportunities for walking in worship, practicing in prayer, and working out in the Word, what are some barriers that keep you from moving forward in these areas? As you have spent time exercising your faith, what has God revealed to your heart?

4) Are you starting to find some muscle groups you have not exercised in awhile? What emotions or fears come to mind as you think about ways to build spiritual muscle? If you have built spiritual muscle in areas of your walk with God, are there any weak spots? Are there muscles you rely on more than others that might be overshadowing some weaker muscle groups?

# OXYGEN
## The Breath of Life

Okay, take a deep breath. Over the last four chapters we have spent quite a bit of time looking at habits, some good and some not so good. We've talked about things that distract us from God and keep us from our full potential as men. We've also talked about our eating and exercise habits. Guarding your heart is not about keeping a list of dos and don'ts, but it is about taking some time to look deeply at our hearts to receive from God a clear calling to his mission. Now we need to take some time to discover the how to breathe again and to tap back into the source of oxygen we need to sustain *life*, not just survive.

## Drive and Overactivity

You may find it difficult in the midst of day-to-day life to take time to really discover, or rather uncover, your heart. Without disconnecting with the drive of life, you may never be able to get at your heart to understand the passion that drives you. Gary Smalley and John Trent state this point very well in their book *The Gift of The Blessing*. The same drive keeps us from being able to share a blessing or quality time with our families.

> In the United States we live in a culture that is so "fast paced" that it makes it easy to be "driven" to the breaking point." A thief is loose in many homes today who masquerades as "fulfillment," "accomplishment," and "success." Actually, this thief steals the precious gift of genuine acceptance from our children and leaves confusion and emptiness in its place. That villain's name is overactivity, and it can keep parents so busy that the blessing is never spoken. Even with parents who dearly love their children, as one woman we talked to said, "Who has time to stop and tell them?"
>
> In many homes today, both parents are working overtime, and a "family night" makes an appearance about as often as Halley's comet. The result is that instead of Dad and Mom taking the time to communicate a spoken blessing, a babysitter named silence is left to mold a child's self-perception. Life is so hectic that for many parents, that "just right" time to communicate a spoken blessing never quite comes around.
>
> *The Gift of the Blessing, pages 33–34*

Now, stop and exhale—or for those of you who are presently hyperventilating, grab a paper bag. Let's look into the very Breath of Life that we need to survive and live lives that shower blessings on us and our families.

## Taking Time to Breathe

We all need oxygen to survive. Our heart requires it for every beat it makes. Oxygen is an essential nutrient in everything we do. Did you know that approximately 65 percent of the human body is made up of oxygen in various molecular structures? Without oxygen, it is impossible to sustain life. How is it that a completely colorless, odorless, and tasteless gas could have such a vital role in our day-to-day lives? It is not something we can see or create or completely understand. We must simply breath it in.

Jesus tells us that we must have childlike faith. The very amazing and very real part of his message is that we must learn to abide in him, every breath of every moment of every day must be spent walking with him, talking with him, and being with him.

Every parent knows the joy of seeing their first child born. There is great anticipation for the day that child is to be born, the moment the child is no longer inside the mother's womb but instead is birthed into this world surrounded by air and no longer to be surrounded by the water in the womb. That moment the head first appears as it is delivered is a moment of indescribable amazement. A new life has come into the world. But to survive, that child has to take a breath…the breath of life. Oxygen is no longer provided through the umbilical cord from the mother. It has to be inspired through the airways and lungs of this new little life. It is a moment when mothers and dads (and doctors for that matter) hold their breath to await the gasp of air and the loud cry of a newborn baby. It is a moment that when the room is quiet, fear grips those in attendance. But once that initial time of transition takes place, life begins outside the womb. Babies begin to breath in oxygen as a very natural process, not out of conscious attempts at trying to make it happen, but out of a very natural created sense of learning to abide in this world.

We also must become like babes once again to come to Christ and to breathe in the Breath of Life—the Holy Spirit. Just as in Ezekiel 37 when God commands Ezekiel to prophesy, "I will make breath enter you and you will come to life" (Ezekiel 37:5, NIV), so the Holy Spirit enters our hearts at the time when we receive Christ to bring us life. Christ is the Breath of Life—he is our very source of spiritual oxygen. He is the vital force in our hearts. He is the essential nutrient in everything we do.

## Of Life and Breath

Without oxygen, our bodies become tired, weary, lethargic, depressed and irritable and our minds are susceptible to poor judgment and irrational thinking; yet when our bodies receive the oxygen they need, our minds are sharp and alert, our bodies are healthy, and we have energy and vitality for life. Unfortunately, most of us do not know what life is like without oxygen. Because we are generally healthy, we have never had a time where we were without the breath of life. Unless you have ever suffered from COPD, or Asthma, or been smothered by your older brother with a big pillow, you do not know how it feels to hunger for oxygen.

Let's do a little exercise. You might want to check with your doctor to make sure it is okay to attempt this. Take a big deep breath and hold it for sixty seconds. How did it feel to go as long as you did without breathing and without oxygen? Not very natural was it?

Now from a spiritual mindset, imagine going your whole life without ever knowing what it was like to have the Breath of Life in you, life without Jesus Christ through the power of the Holy Spirit. How can something that was meant to be such a part of our life (the Breath of Life) be so easy for us to get along without?

## Our Vital Force

A quote from A.B. Simpson is used in *Tozer on the Holy Spirit* on April 24th:

> The Holy Spirit is an infinite force that makes our life powerful, and enables us to accomplish all for which we are called as disciples of Christ. It is power over sin, power over self, power over the world … power to be, to do.

But sometimes we have to make the conscious decision to breathe! We must train ourselves to go back over and over again each day to Jesus, the source of life and learn to abide in him, to find that we are truly living and truly abiding.

As adults we seem to be wired backwards. We have

to learn to consciously breathe like a child to live as disciples of Christ. It takes work and devotion and determination and desire. And yet one day when we least realize or expect it, we find that we are partaking in the *Breath of Life*, as naturally as a child. No longer are we consciously attempting to abide, but the life of Christ is abiding in us through his Holy Spirit. We find that the very delight of our lives has become the desire of our heart.

From the time we receive Christ, the power of the Holy Spirit and all the blessings that come through the work of the cross are ours. But it can take us awhile to get it, to figure out that we do not have to do life on our own strength. We are men after all, and we know how to do this, right? Why do we need to look to someone else for instructions or directions?

## Great and Unsearchable Things

In Jeremiah 33:3 (NIV), the Lord tells Jeremiah, "Call to me and I will answer you and tell you great and unsearchable things you do not know." Are you ready for the instructions yet? Did you think you could just come to God to get a simple answer, not really looking for the great and unsearchable things? Yet that is the power of Christ in us. We are no longer called to do things in the ordinary way because the ordinary way failed to keep us close to God. No the Holy Spirit has come to instruct us in *supernatural* ways. He leads us back home. He replaces our lack of desire with the very desire of our heart. Recall Romans 5:8

(NIV)? "But God demonstrates his own love for us in this: While we were still sinners, Christ died for us."

Think back to when you first came to Christ. That day you asked Jesus in your heart was the very first day of the rest of your life. Jesus did not die on the cross just so you could know him for one day or one occasion. But the Holy Spirit has been at work, first drawing you to Christ, and now to continue to work in and through you, that every day would be a new occasion to love him more deeply, more intimately. Ephesians 2:10 (NIV) says, "For we are God's workmanship, created in Christ Jesus to do good works, which God prepared in advance for us to do." Even before he called you, he had a plan in mind for you. It was prepared in advance.

Is it any wonder that we cannot understand our hearts without the help of the Holy Spirit? He has planted deep within us the desires of our heart, a workmanship of the soul, great and unsearchable things. He is that *treasure* planted in our hearts that sustains us. And as he reveals to us the good works that God had in mind for us to do as we draw close to him, we are transformed. We recognize that we are part of a much bigger story. Every role is vital. Our hearts awaken as the reality of what we know from God's Word stirs our minds, our hearts, and our emotions. The Holy Spirit begins to unearth that deep yearning that we recognize as ours in him. It is as if we are given a new name, a name that we have never heard before but somewhere in the depths of our hearts it is familiar. We step into that name. We step out in faith to enter the battle. We fight to bring the One who called us honor and glory.

If you open your Bible to Acts chapter 2, you get a sense of what the disciples discovered. They had known and walked with Jesus for over three years, but it was not until Pentecost that their lives were transformed. Simon Peter discovered his new name, the rock on which Jesus would build His church. Peter had no idea of the combustive power of the Breath of Life until the Holy Spirit took over his heart.

When the day of Pentecost came, they were all together in one place. Suddenly a sound like the blowing of a violent wind came from heaven and filled the whole house where they were sitting. They saw what seemed to be tongues of fire that separated and came to rest on each of them. All of them were filled with the Holy Spirit and began to speak in other tongues as the Spirit enabled them.

Then Peter stood up with the Eleven, raised his voice and addressed the crowd: "Fellow Jews and all of you who live in Jerusalem, let me explain this to you; listen carefully to what I say. These men are not drunk, as you suppose. It's only nine in the morning! No, this is what was spoken by the prophet Joel:

"'In the last days, God says, I will pour out my Spirit on all people. Your sons and daughters will prophesy, your young men will see visions, your old men will dream dreams. Even on my servants, both men and women, I will pour out my Spirit in those days, and they will prophesy. I will show wonders in the heaven above and signs on the earth below, blood and fire and billows of smoke. The sun will be turned to darkness and the moon to blood before the coming of the great and glorious day of the Lord. And everyone who calls on the name of the Lord will be saved.'"

Those who accepted his message were baptized, and about three thousand were added to their number that day.

Acts 2:1–4, 14–21, 41 (NIV)

Remember Peter? It had not been all that long ago that he denied knowing Christ three times prior to the death of Jesus. After Jesus was resurrected, he came to Peter, who just happened to be out fishing again, and asked him to "Feed [his] sheep" (John 21:17, NIV). Do you think Peter was catching on yet? Suddenly there was a mighty wind, tongues of fire, an anointing and filling with the Holy Spirit. Peter spoke with boldness and prophesied because he recognized who he was, not in his own power but in the power of the Holy Spirit. He had not learned some new language in a listening lab and linguistics class. It was imparted to him when the Holy Spirit came upon him. And at nine in the morning, some three thousand were added to the flock of the early church. How was Peter able to accomplish this? "Not by might, not by power, but by my Spirit," says the Lord" (Zechariah 4:6, NIV).

We should not be surprised at the power of the Holy Spirit that was poured out upon God's people. Jesus tells us in John in several instances that he had to go so that the Holy Spirit could come.

But I tell you the truth: It is for your good that I am going away. Unless I go away, the Counselor

will not come to you; but if I go, I will send him
to you...I have much more to say to you, more
than you can now bear. But when he, the Spirit of
truth, comes, he will guide you into all truth. He
will not speak on his own; he will speak only what
he hears, and he will tell you what is yet to come.
He will bring glory to me by taking from what is
mine and making it known to you.

John 16: 7, 12–14 (NIV)

Jesus ascended into heaven after the Resurrection. The
Holy Spirit descended at the time of Pentecost. And now
we have a Counselor, the Spirit of Truth, the One True
Guide, the very voice of God to talk with us and draw
us near to the heart of God. He places that desire in our
heart. It is not something that we can dig up and produce.
The Holy Spirit takes our broken bodies, which in the
natural realm, want to run from God; yet, in the spiritual
realm he transforms us supernaturally to be sons of God.

But the Counselor, the Holy Spirit, whom the
Father will send in my name, will teach you all
things and will remind you of everything I have
said to you.

John 14:26 (NIV)

On the evening of that first day of the week, when
the disciples were together, with the doors locked for
fear of the Jews, Jesus came and stood among them
and said, "Peace be with you!" After he said this, he
showed them his hands and side. The disciples were
overjoyed when they saw the Lord. Again Jesus said,

> "Peace be with you! As the Father has sent me, I am
> sending you." And with that he breathed on them
> and said, "Receive the Holy Spirit."
>
> John 20:19–22 (NIV)

Jesus knew the plan the Father had drawn up. Abraham
had offered up his son Isaac, and Isaac was spared. This
time Jesus was being offered up by God the Father, but
there was no other way out. Jesus knew his role and knew
the only way out was through suffering on the cross. Yet
God's divine plan did not end on the cross, nor at the
Resurrection, nor at Pentecost, nor today, nor does it ever
end. But Jesus knew that he was not to be the Counselor.
That job was designed by God the Father for the Holy
Spirit to seal those who would receive Christ in their
hearts and to guide them back to the Father. He would
bestow on them a new name, for each had become a new
creation, a workmanship, sons of God.

> And you also were included in Christ when you
> heard the word of truth, the gospel of your sal-
> vation. Having believed, you were marked in him
> with a seal, the promised Holy Spirit, who is a
> deposit guaranteeing our inheritance until the re-
> demption of those who are God's possession–to
> the praise of his glory.
>
> Ephesians 1:13–14 (NIV)

There is a very important identity that each of us carry around
in our wallets on our driver's license. We see our picture and
notice our birth date. On that date we were named. We took

on the name of our earthly father, or through adoption took on the last name of the man we recognize as our dad. It is the name by which we are commonly known.

And now we have a new identity, an identity in Christ. We have been given a new name and sealed by the Holy Spirit with a name that is written in the Book of Life. God the Father has made you his son, and in him you have life and breath and hope and honor. Are you like Peter? Think you can only ever be just another fisherman? Let the Holy Spirit unearth that which is hidden, unsearchable things, deep desires, the treasure bestowed upon you.

Follow in Peter's footprints and allow the Holy Spirit to awaken and transform you with his power, to make you into a solid rock for the kingdom of God. You do not have to look beyond the four walls of your own home to know he has destined you for glory. You are to be a great influence on the generations that follow. He is able to do it as you abide with him and in him. *He has called you by name.* God is calling. Rise up man of God. The kingdom awaits you. Your destination of desire is upon you.

## Verses to Ponder

> Guard the good deposit that was entrusted to you—guard it with the help of the Holy Spirit who lives in us.
>
> 2 Timothy 1:14 (NIV)

> We put no stumbling block in anyone's path, so that our ministry will not be discredited. Rather, as servants of God we commend ourselves in every

way: in great endurance; in troubles, hardships and distresses; in beatings, imprisonments and riots; in hard work, sleepless nights and hunger; in purity, understanding, patience and kindness; in the Holy Spirit and in sincere love; in truthful speech and in the power of God; with weapons of righteousness in the right hand and in the left; through glory and dishonor, bad report and good report; genuine, yet regarded as impostors; known, yet regarded as unknown; dying, and yet we live on; beaten, and yet not killed; sorrowful, yet always rejoicing; poor, yet making many rich; having nothing, and yet possessing everything.

2 Corinthians 6:3–10 (NIV)

## Pulse Check

1) As you take time to take a step back and look at your life, are there areas where overactivity plagues you? Why are you so driven in this area? Do you feel disconnected from God in this area? How does it disconnect you from your family? What steps can you take to reduce this over-activity?

2) Do you remember when your first child was born? What was amazing to you about that moment or about the first time you met them? Did it make you stop and think about life for a moment? What areas of your spiritual heart need to have the Breath of Life breathed into them?

3) What was life like before you met Christ and allowed the Holy Spirit to enter your heart? Do you remember the day you accepted Jesus Christ into your heart? Where do

you sense the Holy Spirit leading you now? What things is he asking you to let go of?

4) Take some time to look at Peter's life again. Jesus turns and ordinary fisherman into a fisher of men during his time on earth. Yet after Jesus dies on the cross, Peter returns to his life as a fisherman. How is your walk with Jesus? Are you trying to go back to the old ways of life or are you being transformed into the rock that Jesus wants you to become through the power of the Holy Spirit?

# PACEMAKER
## Passions of the Heart

Right now inside everyone's heart there is a little grouping of cells that fires an electrical signal that tells the heart to beat. It is not something we think about or try to consciously control, it just happens. It is part of how we were created, our innate nature. The only time we ever really get worried about this pacemaker within our heart is when it is not working like it is supposed to. If it does not produce beats, or it conducts those beats abnormally, we label it sick sinus syndrome. If another pathway starts firing above or near these special cells, our heart beats too fast. In either instance, we tend to not feel well. We are either on the verge of passing out when we stand up and feel terribly sluggish, or we feel like our heart is going to beat out of our chest and cannot seem to catch our breath.

God has designed the pacemaker in our hearts to help keep pace with our day-to-day activities. While we sleep, it might only beat sixty times a minute (or slower if you are an athlete). Yet when we are awake, it keeps up with the moment-by-moment demands of our every move. When we go for a jog, it speeds up. When we are at rest, it settles down. When we jump up from our chair and dash across the room to answer the phone, it speeds up.

## Gifts, Talents and Abilities

God has also created us with certain innate qualities. You might refer to them as gifts or talents or abilities. Regardless of what you might name them, God has named us by them. Yes we are all created very similarly, man and woman, with typical features and qualities that make us men or women. But we are not just a bunch of look-alikes thrown from the same mold. No, God looked down on each of us as we were formed and began to grow in us distinct gifts and talents and abilities that only we possess. He knew these things would bring us life and allow us to function just right. And he chose this time to put us here for us to use our gifts, talents, and abilities in front of a world that would be watching for such a time as this.

Think about it for a second. How are you known? Are you a handy man? Plumber? Architect? Doctor? Mechanic? Teacher? Are you known by your ability to discern situations and make right decisions? Your ability to design and create something from a blank piece of paper? Your ability to listen and really get into people's hearts? Your compassion, your ability to put others first, your childlike faith, your tender heart, your ability to work with your hands and fix anything?

Look back at the Old Testament to Moses' time and the tent of meeting. Although Moses was the leader of the Israelites and the one called to lead them up out of Egypt, he relied upon the people to bring the offering of gold, silver, bronze, linen, hides, and goat hair to help build the tent of meeting. And he was also not gifted with the skills, abilities, or knowledge with crafts, but he knew a couple guys that were.

> Then Moses said to the Israelites, "See, the Lord has chosen Bezalel son of Uri, the son of Hur, of the tribe of Judah, and he has filled him with the Spirit of God, with skill, ability and knowledge in all kinds of crafts—to make artistic designs for work in gold, silver and bronze, to cut and set stones, to work in wood and to engage in all kinds of artistic craftsmanship. And he has given both him and Oholiab son of Ahisamach, of the tribe of Dan, the ability to teach others. He has filled them with skill to do all kinds of work as crafts-men, designers, embroiderers in blue, purple and scarlet yarn and fine linen, and weavers—all of them master craftsmen and designers..."
>
> Exodus 35:30–35 (NIV)

These men may have served in a rather *ordinary* capacity up until this time in their lives, but spending so much time doing *ordinary* things with gold, silver, stones, wood, embroidery, weaving, and designing allowed them to be called to do *extraordinary* things for God at just the right time in their lives. No one else was so skilled as to be able to accomplish these tasks. No one else was able to teach others as these men could. And God used these regular guys to create a Most Holy Place for the Most High.

Webster's defines a talent as "a characteristic feature, aptitude, or disposition of a person; the natural endowments of a person; a special often athletic, creative, or artistic aptitude." (Merriam-Webster.com, "talent") And ability is "competence in doing; natural aptitude or acquired proficiency." (Merriam-Webster.com, "ability") So do you see it yet? Can you sense that God has created you for such a time as this? It's not necessarily about pride in being able to perform better than most, it's about God-given talent to be used to his glory to advance his kingdom. No one else can do what you can with the skill and competence that God gave to you.

## The Messengers and the Message

So what do some of these things look like? Paul discusses this a little in Ephesians 4, but for all of these different types of ministry to succeed, there has to be a whole village of people undergirding the ministry with their support. Think of it like a big basketball arena. To get to the game you pass people that direct you to park, collect your tickets, sell you concessions and memorabilia, show you to your seat, announce what is going on in the game, etc. There is a very clear direction to help you focus your attention on the game. Without it you'd be stuck in traffic. God has also given very clear direction to his messengers.

> It was he who gave some to be apostles, some to be
> prophets, some to be evangelists, and some to be pas-
> tors and teachers, to prepare God's people for works
> of service, so that the body of Christ may be built up
> until we all reach unity in the faith and in the knowl-
> edge of the Son of God and become mature, attain-
> ing to the whole measure of the fullness of Christ.
>
> Ephesians 4:11–13 (NIV)

We have a tendency to look at the apostles, prophets, evangelists, pastors, and teachers as such amazing people who serve God, and they are. But let's not forget about who invited us to the revival ceremony, or who invited us to church, or who will be there every day for us after we receive our salvation—brothers, sisters, family, friends, neighbors. That is why Paul exhorts us in Colossians 3:23–24 (NIV): "Whatever you do, work at it with all your heart, as working for the Lord, not for men, since you know that you will receive an inheritance from the Lord as a reward. It is the Lord Christ you are serving."

In this way, we can look to God for our reward for being faithful and as we do, the eyes of our co-workers will be on us ever-wondering why it is we work with such joy despite it being hard work. Why are we able to put up with so much? We are working for the Lord.

Yet even in our day-to-day jobs, Christ promises to be there with us. He has given us his seal through the Holy Spirit. And as the Holy Spirit is revealed, we begin to walk in love, joy, peace, patience, kindness, goodness, and self-control (the fruit of our labor). I love the way

Paul writes to the Corinthians about the matters of gifts, service, and work.

> There are different kinds of gifts, but the same Spirit. There are different kinds of service, but the same Lord. There are different kinds of working, but the same God works all of them in all men. Now to each one the manifestation of the Spirit is given for the common good. To one there is given through the Spirit the message of wisdom, to another the message of knowledge by means of the same Spirit, to another faith by the same Spirit, to another gifts of healing by that one Spirit, to another miraculous powers, to another prophecy, to another distinguishing between spirits, to another speaking in different kinds of tongues, and to still another the interpretation of tongues. All these are the work of one and the same Spirit, and he gives them to each one, just as he determines.
>
> 1 Corinthians 12:4–11 (NIV)

## Discovering the Gifts Within

So what is it that really makes your heart beat—that thing that comes as easy to you as breathing? What is it that everybody knows you are not just good at but *great*? Are there some hidden talents you have yet to discover? Press toward God and allow him to show you just what gifts he has determined to give you, skills, and abilities, and opportunities of service that will allow the Holy Spirit of God to work in and through you. Step out and affect the lives of people all around you. Don't hold back.

"Again, it will be like a man going on a journey, who called his servants and entrusted his property to them. To one he gave five talents of money, to another two talents, and to another one talent, each according to his ability. Then he went on his journey. The man who had received the five talents went at once and put his money to work and gained five more. So also, the one with the two talents gained two more. But the man who had received the one talent went off, dug a hole in the ground and hid his master's money.

"After a long time the master of those servants returned and settled accounts with them. The man who had received the five talents brought the other five. 'Master,' he said, 'you entrusted me with five talents. See, I have gained five more.'

"His master replied, 'Well done, good and faithful servant! You have been faithful with a few things; I will put you in charge of many things. Come and share your master's happiness!'

"The man with the two talents also came. 'Master,' he said, 'you entrusted me with two talents; see, I have gained two more.'

"His master replied, 'Well done, good and faithful servant! You have been faithful with a few things; I will put you in charge of many things. Come and share your master's happiness!'

"Then the man who had received the one talent came. 'Master,' he said, 'I knew that you are a hard man, harvesting where you have not sown and gathering where you have not scattered seed. So I was afraid and went out and hid your talent in the ground. See, here is what belongs to you.'

"His master replied, 'You wicked, lazy servant! So you knew that I harvest where I have not sown and gather where I have not scattered seed? Well then, you should have put my money on deposit with the bankers, so that when I returned I would have received it back with interest.

"'Take the talent from him and give it to the one who has the ten talents. For everyone who has will be given more, and he will have an abundance. Whoever does not have, even what he has will be taken from him.'"

Matthew 25:14–29 (NIV)

## The One Who Gives

Have you discovered your gifts, who you are, and how God has brought you to this place and this time for a very specific purpose? God so wants us to discover those gifts, but we have to start with discovering him. He wants to be the ultimate desire of our hearts and until we get to that point, our gifts, talents, and abilities look rather pointless. Let's stop again and look into the book of Jeremiah.

"For I know the plans I have for you," declares the Lord, "plans to prosper you and not to harm you, plans to give you hope and a future."

Jeremiah 29:11 (NIV)

What does it mean to prosper in God's terms? Is it merely being fortunate and successful or rather does it mean that we thrive, grow vigorously, and flourish? So what does it take to grow and flourish? To prosper on God's terms, we cannot starve ourselves spiritually. We need the Bread of Life *daily*. We need to have our thirst quenched with Living Water. God desires that we would desire him. He has plans in mind to give you hope and a future. We just need to ask, seek, and knock, to discover who we are, who we are meant to be, who God is, and find life welling up from within our hearts.

> If you make the Most High your dwelling—
>     even the Lord, who is my refuge—
>     then no harm will befall you,
>     no disaster will come near your tent.
>     For he will command his angels concerning you
>     to guard you in all your ways;
>     they will lift you up in their hands,
>     so that you will not strike your foot against a stone.
>     You will tread upon the lion and the cobra;
>     you will trample the great lion and the serpent.
>     "Because he loves me," says the Lord, "I will
> rescue him;
>     I will protect him, for he acknowledges my name.
>     He will call upon me, and I will answer him;
>     I will be with him in trouble,
>     I will deliver him and honor him.
>     With long life will I satisfy him
>     and show him my salvation."
>                                   Psalm 91:9–16 (NIV)

## Getting There?

With each step along the way, he not only sustains us but he knows the steps we will take even before we take them.

Unfortunately, we also think we know what steps we need to be taking to get from point A to point B. Sometimes we prefer a straight line (God get me there *now*), but God might have a different design. He is interested in the *process*. He is more interested in growing us and drawing us near to him, and using circumstances to teach us to trust him and grow our faith, than he is with whether or not our plans succeed. He indwells us with strength not necessarily for our desire and purposes to be carried out and not necessarily for self-preservation either.

Jesus calls us to "take up the cross…lay down your life…abide in me." As we do this we discover our Maker and find that his plans and his perfect design for our lives far exceeds anything we could ever imagine. Talents we never knew we possessed become traits in our lives by which we are identified, our calling, our name by which he calls us, the very nature that drives our beating heart.

## Verses to ponder

> Then he said to them all: "If anyone would come after me, he must deny himself and take up his cross daily and follow me. For whoever wants to save his life will lose it, but whoever loses his life for me will save it. What good is it for a man to gain the whole world, and yet lose or forfeit his very self?
>
> Luke 9:23–25 (NIV)

> Greater love has no one than this, that he lay down his life for his friends.
>
> John 15:13 (NIV)

"I am the true vine, and my Father is the garden-
er. He cuts off every branch that doesn't produce
fruit, and he prunes the branches that do bear fruit
so they will produce even more. You have already
been pruned for greater fruitfulness by the message I have given you. Remain (Abide) in me, and
I will remain in you. For a branch cannot produce
fruit if it is severed from the vine, and you cannot
be fruitful apart from me. Yes, I am the vine; you
are the branches. Those who remain (abide) in me,
and I in them, will produce much fruit. For apart
from me you can do nothing."

John 15:1–5 (NLT)

## Pulse Check

1) What passion drives your heart? What are you good
at and what do you enjoy doing? If you've not taken a
spiritual gifts assessment, that may be something worth
checking into, especially if you have questions about your
spiritual giftedness. How can you use your passion and
gifts to serve God?

2) What was the last major sporting event or concert that
you went to? How many people wearing "Event Staff"
jackets did you pass by? As you think of the church, what
role do you play in supporting your local church? What
"Event Staff" jacket do you wear?

3) Is your passion for God growing? What are you asking God, seeking his direction in, knocking at his door

for? Do you find your desires changing or becoming more focused as you lay those passions before God?

4) Are you a process oriented or a goal driven person? Does it make you uneasy to be clay in God's hands, maybe not knowing what the end result might be? Stop for a minute and close your eyes. As you listen to God speaking to your heart, what do you hear him saying to you right now? What is the special name that he calls you by? Write it down and never forget it.

# THE BODY

## Brotherhood in Action

The human body is amazingly designed. Yet to function as it is supposed to, God has established at the very core, the human heart. Without it being healthy, everything else in the body is affected. Over the course of this book we have talked about distractions and stressors; wounds and healing; feeding on the Bread of Life; exercising our faith in worship, prayer, time in the Word, and solitude; the Holy Spirit as our vital supply of life- and the very strength God has placed in our hearts, talents, abilities, and gifts. God's design supersedes the human heart. His ultimate goal is for us to know and to enjoy him and to battle for the lives of others to join the King's army. Just as we have been called, many more are to soon become sons and daughters of the Most High and that is by his design. Each of us has been created uniquely for our role in the body of Christ. All of life's toils, strains, wounds and sorrows, joys, adventures, triumphs, and victories have each had a role in preparing us for today and for the days ahead—to carry out God's purposes in our lives. Read the words of Paul to the Corinthians in his first letter chapter 12:

> The human body has many parts, but the many parts make up only one body. So it is with the body of Christ. Some of us are Jews, some are Gentiles, some are slaves, and some are free. But we have all been baptized into Christ's body by one Spirit, and we have all received the same Spirit.
>
> Yes, the body has many different parts, not just one part. If the foot says, "I am not a part of the body because I am not a hand," that does not make it any less a part of the body. And if the ear says, "I am not part of the body because I am only an ear and not an eye," would that make it any less a part of the body? Suppose the whole body were an eye—then how would you hear? Or if your whole body were just one big ear, how could you smell anything?
>
> But God made our bodies with many parts, and he has put each part just where he wants it. What a strange thing a body would be if it had only one part! Yes, there are many parts, but only one body. The eye can never say to the hand, "I don't need you." The head can't say to the feet, "I don't need you."
>
> In fact, some of the parts that seem weakest and least important are really the most necessary. And the parts we regard as less honorable are those we clothe with the greatest care. So we carefully protect from the eyes of others those parts that should not be seen, while other parts do not require this special care. So God has put the body

together in such a way that extra honor and care are given to those parts that have less dignity. This makes for harmony among the members, so that all the members care for each other equally. If one part suffers, all the parts suffer with it, and if one part is honored, all the parts are glad.

Now all of you together are Christ's body, and each one of you is a separate and necessary part of it. Here is a list of some of the members that God has placed in the body of Christ: first are apostles, second are prophets, third are teachers, then those who do miracles, those who have the gift of healing, those who can help others, those who can get others to work together, those who speak in unknown languages.

Is everyone an apostle? Of course not. Is everyone a prophet? No. Are all teachers? Does everyone have the power to do miracles? Does everyone have the gift of healing? Of course not. Does God give all of us the ability to speak in unknown languages? Can everyone interpret unknown languages? No! And in any event, you should desire the most helpful gifts. First, however, let me tell you about something else that is better than any of them!

1 Corinthians 12:12–31 (NLT)

Did you hear that? God has placed you right where you are for such a time as this. Though we serve separate roles, we are never alone. Never allow Satan to devalue where God has given value to you. Let's look again to John 10:10 (NIV): "The thief comes only to steal and kill and destroy; I have come that they may have life, and have it to the full."

Satan's ultimate plan is to steal from God and from

you, to kill you and anything that God views as life, and to destroy any hopes you have for attaining to something great. But remember who won our victory at the cross on Calvary. Whose shed blood has bought us at the highest price? Who overcame death and the grave? Who sits at the right hand of the Father now glorified? Jesus.

## Living Abundantly

Some translations use the word abundantly at the end of John 10:10 (NASB) "have life, and have it abundantly." So what is abundance? Several other terms define the word abundant. These same terms could be inserted here at the end of the verse—*fully sufficient, plentiful, richly supplied, bountiful, exuberant, profuse, overflowing, teeming.* (Merriam-Webster.com, "abundant") Did you catch that? Jesus does not say that we would have just a little life or just enough life or maybe some extra life on special days! No, he gives us *life* overflowing, teeming from within. Jesus did not stay dead at the cross; he rose to life. He has not called us to follow him to the foot of the cross and stay there as though dead! He wants us to rise to life and live with abundance!

Oswald Chamber makes just such a statement in *My Upmost For His Highest.*

> "Consider the lilies of the field, how they grow: they neither toil nor spin"—they simply are! Jesus said there is only one way to develop and grow spiritually, and that is through focusing and concentrating on God. In other words, pay attention to the Source, and out of you "will flow rivers of

living water" (John 7:38). Our heavenly Father knows our circumstances, and if we will stay focused on Him, instead of our circumstances, we will grow spiritually—just as "the lilies of the field."
    Entry from *My Upmost For His Highest*, May 18

Oswald Chamber blows me away time after time with his simple yet poignant wisdom regarding the Word of God. Look to the lilies. I'm not talking about the fresh cut flowers you see in the grocery store that you buy your wife to save your keister after you forgot her birthday or your anniversary. You may not stop very often to look at flowers. There may not be lilies around, but if you happen to be driving across the countryside, look along the road at the wildflowers that grow. Think about the cold winter or the hot summer, the rain, snow, heat and sun, the complete exposure to the elements, to road salt, to beasts of the field, and to errant tire tracks. And yet they still *are!* Are you ready yet to put it all down and drop the facade before God? Just take some time to be his son. He would love to just spend some time with you not *doing* anything. Just be still ... and know that he is your Father ... and you are his son. Didn't know there could be so much life in just doing nothing did you?

## Being a Jonathan

Jesus is all about life and he wants to share it with us and in turn he wants us to share it with others. No, I'm not saying you are necessarily called to be a prophet or an evangelist or a pastor, but I do think you are called to be a Jonathan. Read the verses below and you will see what I am getting at.

David stayed in the desert strongholds and in the hills in the Desert of Ziph. Day after day Saul searched for him, but God did not give David into his hands. While David was at Horesh in the Desert of Ziph, he learned that Saul had come out to take his life. And Saul's son Jonathan went to David at Horesh and *helped him find strength in God* (emphasis mine). "Don't be afraid," he said. "My father Saul will not lay a hand on you. You will be king over Israel, and I will be second to you. Even my father Saul knows this." The two of them made a covenant before the Lord. Then Jonathan went home, but David remained at Horesh.

1 Samuel 23: 14–18 (NIV)

The ministry of Jonathan is necessary, and it is important. He brought King David great comfort and encouragement as he feared for his life and waited on God's timing in the middle of a desert. He was alone, likely discouraged, and maybe about ready to give up on all that God had placed in his heart. But Jonathan reminded him of God's promises. He reminded him of who he was. God is our warrior and defender. *He named you, and you will be great.* David was to be a king. Jonathan was a true friend to David. Jonathan served the king well. Jonathan took the risk to go to his friend, a risk that could cost him his life (Saul had already slung several spears Jonathan's way). Jonathan helped to revive David back to life. He helped him get his heart back.

Do you know someone like that? Maybe they are just waiting for someone to come along beside them and give them those few words of encouragement that helps them get back into the fight. Or maybe there are a few guys that you have been meeting with for coffee or a Bible study. Have you ever recognized the importance of those times you have spent together? Maybe it has never been anything more than superficial friendships, but have you ever hoped to be able to dig deeper? It may be that everyone is simply waiting for the invitation. Are you willing to step out in faith to deepen those bonds of brotherhood?

## Of Sheep and Sheep Pens

I want to take you on a little journey for a bit. It might be somewhat of a sidetrack, but I think there is a point worth making here. Take a look at John 10 and the truth of what Jesus shares in the following verses.

> I tell you the truth, the man who does not enter the sheep pen by the gate, but climbs in by some other way, is a thief and a robber. The man who enters by the gate is the shepherd of his sheep. The watchman opens the gate for him, and the sheep listen to his voice. He calls his own sheep by name and leads them out. When he has brought out all his own, he goes on ahead of them, and his sheep follow him because they know his voice.
>
> John 10:1–4 (NIV)

Most of us marvel at the parables of Jesus, and this is another that catches us by surprise. We recognize the contrast Jesus shares between the Good Shepherd and the thief. We stand in awe that he calls us out by his own voice and there is a deep sense of trust as we follow after him. But go back to the passage and take note of the sheep (us). We are all in the same sheep pen. We all are witnesses to how the days and nights pass here. The Watchman (Holy Spirit) is here with us, and yet the thief will still try to enter by some other way. We know our Shepherd's voice. We all recognize it. And we know he will someday lead us out of this sheep pen to a beautiful meadow to enjoy with him.

The point is not to belittle us into believing that we are merely sheep to just be led around and be dulled by all of life. The point is that we are in this pen *together*. We all face very similar circumstances. Sometimes we need those around us to point us in the direction of the Good Shepherd, especially when the noise around us seems to distract us from his voice (mentoring). We need to know others will be there to warn us if they see something deceptive going on and to defend us if the enemy is trying to enter the sheep pen (fighting for our faith). As the Savior leads us out, the herd gets moving even if it means getting kicked and pushed back in the Savior's direction (loving rebuke). And maybe it is the voice of the flock in unison that cries out to get the attention of our loving Savior (intercession). Remember, he was there in the pen with us as a lowly lamb, and he is not unaware of all that goes on here. It's not like the sheep pen is the cleanest, roomiest, most fragrant place to hang out. But to God, "we are the aroma of Christ" (2 Corinthians 2:15, NIV).

## Bearing Arms

We are each called to bear arms, spiritually speaking, and to fight for the kingdom, for our Father, and on behalf of our brothers and sisters in Christ. Knights of the Round Table fought and lived together for the sake of the kingdom of King Arthur. They each lived by a code of chivalry which included to never do outrage or murder, always to flee treason, to by no means be cruel but to give mercy unto him who asks for mercy, to always do ladies, gentlewomen, and widows succor, to never force ladies, gentlewomen or widows, and not to take up battles in wrongful quarrels for love or worldly goods. The Winchester Round Table at which they met had no head or foot, thereby representing the equality of all the members. (Wikipedia.org, "Knights of the Round Table")

I'm not asking you to live by a code of chivalry. God has a higher standard. Yet even with such a superficial code of conduct, King Arthur's knights lived valiantly for noble and earthly purposes. But our vision is fixed on heaven and the higher calling God has placed on us. Life here on earth passes like a vapor, but eternity will never pass. Have you found a few good men? Are you ready to make that transition from self-preservation to fighting for a cause beyond all earthly treasure?

> A final word: Be strong with the Lord's mighty power. Put on all of God's armor so that you will be able to stand firm against all strategies and tricks of the Devil. For we are not fighting against people made of flesh and blood, but against the

evil rulers and authorities of the unseen world, against those mighty powers of darkness who rule this world, and against wicked spirits in the heavenly realms. Use every piece of God's armor to resist the enemy in the time of evil, so that after the battle you will still be standing firm. Stand your ground, putting on the sturdy belt of truth and the body armor of God's righteousness. For shoes, put on the peace that comes from the Good News, so that you will be fully prepared. In every battle you will need faith as your shield to stop the fiery arrows aimed at you by Satan. Put on salvation as your helmet, and take the sword of the Spirit, which is the word of God. Pray at all times and on every occasion in the power of the Holy Spirit. Stay alert and be persistent in your prayers for all Christians everywhere.

Ephesians 6:10–18 (NLT)

## The Fight Worth Fighting

"Religion that God our Father accepts as pure and faultless is this: to look after orphans and widows in their distress and to keep oneself from being polluted by the world" (James 1:27, NIV). Two thoughts: (1) Mission and (2) Guarding your heart. This verse in James shoots it pretty straight and helps us hone down our focus. Pure and faultless religion has these two things in common—mission and guarding our hearts—which we will explore below.

As you look at this verse there are two main encouragements. The first is keeping your eyes open to those around you that need your time, support, influence, encouragement, care, and nurture. All throughout the Bible you read about God's heart for those viewed as weak or as under-dogs. They need someone to fight for them, and time after time God does. Go back to Genesis and read the story of Hagar and Ishmael after they were sent away by Abraham. Look in 2 Samuel at the boy named Mephibosheth, the son of Jonathan, and how David treated him as one of his own sons. Recall how Jesus had mercy on the woman caught in adultery: not one of her accusers threw a stone. Look in the mirror and remember who you were before God's mercy fell on you. God loves to play the hero, to bind up the brokenhearted and give mercy to those in need. And God loves it when his mercy rains through us to reach out to those who need him most in the midst of their distress. We are his hands and his feet.

The second part of the verse is exactly what we have been talking about for the last eight chapters of this book—caring for our hearts. There are so many ways we can become deluded, distracted, misled, and mowed over. We've got to meet with him daily, whether one on one, in corporate worship, or with a group of guys that can tear into us and challenge us to draw upon God. He is our hope.

John Eldredge puts it this way in his book *Wild at Heart*:

> But if you saw your life as a great battle and you *knew* you needed time with God for your very sur-vival, you would do it. Maybe not perfectly—no-body ever does and that's not the point anyway—but you would have a reason to seek him. We give a halfhearted attempt at the spiritual disciplines

when the only reason we have is that we "ought" to. But we'll find a way to make it work when we are convinced we're history if we don't.

Time with God each day is not about academic study or getting through a certain amount of Scripture or any of that. It's about connecting with God. We've got to keep those lines of communication open, so use whatever helps. Sometimes I'll listen to music; other times I'll read Scripture or a passage from a book; often I will journal; maybe I'll go for a run; then there are days when all I need is silence and solitude and the rising sun. The point is simply to do *whatever brings me back to my heart and the heart of God.*

The discipline, by the way, is never the point. The whole point of a "devotional life" is *connecting with God.* This is our primary antidote to the counterfeits the world holds out to us.

*Wild at Heart*, pages 171–172

What does a beating, thriving, passionate, devoted, disciplined, transparent heart look like—one that has the awkward tension of life under control, has bypassed the plagues of the heart, feeds on the Bread of Life, exercises its spiritual muscles, breathes deeply from oxygen tank of Life, and lives passionately with God's purpose and gifting? What this looks like for each of us may be a little different, depending on where we are at in our walk with Christ. The symptoms of living might vary and our circumstances are not the same, but the signs of life are the same. Are we connected with God, grafted into the vine, abiding, and growing? These are signs that we are living life from the inside out with hearts that have been filled with the power of the Holy Spirit.

Each day, circumstances and symptoms will change, but God never changes. All this training and spending time and keeping connected with God is for the purpose of enjoying life as he intended for it to be. To have a heart that is filled to overflowing with life, vibrant and content, this is the purpose for which we were created. And it is not through the *things that were created* that we find this contentment, rather it is by walking in relationship with our *Creator* that we find contentment, vitality, and a heart that beats with purpose. We live to enjoy today to the fullest while at the same time having our eyes focused on the bigger picture—eternity. Paul put it best in his 2nd letter to the Corinthians.

> But we have this treasure in jars of clay to show that this all-surpassing power is from God and not from us. We are hard pressed on every side, but not crushed; perplexed, but not in despair; persecuted, but not abandoned; struck down, but not destroyed. We always carry around in our body the death of Jesus, so that the life of Jesus may also be revealed in our body. For we who are alive are always being given over to death for Jesus' sake, so that his life may be revealed in our mortal body. So then, death is at work in us, but life is at work in you.
>
> Therefore we do not lose heart. Though outwardly we are wasting away, yet inwardly we are being renewed day by day. For our light and momentary troubles are achieving for us an eternal glory that far outweighs them all. So we fix our eyes not

on what is seen, but on what is unseen. For what is
seen is temporary, but what is unseen is eternal.

2 Corinthians 4:7–12, 16–18 (NIV)

Each day we wake up we are given the opportunity to
reconnect on a very deep level with our Creator. He's not
looking for perfection, merely surrender. In place of striving, he offers the gift of adoption as a son. In place of
regret, he offers new life and hope for a bright future. I'll
end our time here with a challenge for a lifetime, and it is
written in 1 Corinthians 13.

> If I speak with the tongues of men and of angels,
> but do not have love, I have become a noisy gong
> or a clanging cymbal. If I have {the gift of} proph-
> ecy, and know all mysteries and all knowledge; and
> if I have all faith, so as to remove mountains, but
> do not have love, I am nothing.
> And if I give all my possessions to feed {the
> poor,} and if I surrender my body to be burned,
> but do not have love, it profits me nothing. Love is
> patient, love is kind {and} is not jealous; love does
> not brag {and} is not arrogant, does not act unbe-
> comingly; it does not seek its own, is not provoked,
> does not take into account a wrong {suffered,} does
> not rejoice in unrighteousness, but rejoices with
> the truth; bears all things, believes all things, hopes
> all things, endures all things. Love never fails; but
> if {there are gifts of} prophecy, they will be done
> away; if {there are} tongues, they will cease; if {there
> is} knowledge, it will be done away. For we know
> in part and we prophesy in part; but when the per-

fect comes, the partial will be done away. When I was a child, I used to speak like a child, think like a child, reason like a child; when I became a man, I did away with childish things. For now we see in a mirror dimly, but then face to face; now I know in part, but then I will know fully just as I also have been fully known. But now faith, hope, love, abide these three; *but the greatest of these is love.*

1 Corinthians 13:1–13 (NASB)

## Verses to Ponder

Peter said to him, "We have left everything to follow you!"

"I tell you the truth," Jesus replied, "no one who has left home or brothers or sisters or mother or father or children or fields for me and the gospel will fail to receive a hundred times as much in this present age (homes, brothers, sisters, mothers, children and fields-and with them, persecutions) and in the age to come, eternal life. But many who are first will be last, and the last first."

Mark 10:28–31 (NIV)

Then Jesus said to his host, "When you give a luncheon or dinner, do not invite your friends, your brothers or relatives, or your rich neighbors; if you do, they may invite you back and so you will be repaid. But when you give a banquet, invite the poor, the cripples, the lame, the blind, and you will be blessed. Although they cannot repay you, you will be repaid at the resurrection of the righteous."

Luke 14:12–14 (NIV)

"Simon, Simon, Satan has asked to sift you as wheat. But I have prayed for you, Simon, that your faith may not fail. And when you have turned back, strengthen your brothers."

Luke 22:31

Therefore, I urge you, brothers, in view of God's mercy, to offer your bodies as living sacrifices, holy and pleasing to God-this is your spiritual act of worship. Do not conform any longer to the pattern of this world, but be transformed by the renewing of your mind. Then you will be able to test and approve what God's will is-his good, pleasing and perfect will.

Be joyful in hope, patient in affliction, faithful in prayer. Share with God's people who are in need. Practice hospitality.

Romans 12:1–2, 12–13 (NIV)

## Pulse Check

1) What thoughts does I Corinthians 12:12–31 invoke in your mind? What role are you called to serve for such a time as this? Where has Satan attempted to devalue your role or destroy your life?

2) What comes to mind as you think of an abundance? Does Oswald Chambers change your view of lilies of the field?

3) As you think about sheep and sheep pens, have you ever appreciated the nudge of another brother to get you headed back in the right direction (back to Christ)? Who can you be a Jonathan to? Are there people God has placed in your path to encourage in the right direction?

4) As we close the last chapter of this book, what feelings or emotions are being stirred within your heart? Do you begin to get the sense of the fight you are in and the fight you are facing when it comes to issues of faith? Are you ready to fight? Can you face the battle with confidence and know that your faith is worth fighting for?

# BIBLIOGRAPHY

Tozer, Aiden Wilson. *Tozer on the Holy Spirit.* Compiled by Marilynne E. Foster. Camp Hill: Christian Publications, Inc., 2000. March 29.

"wellspring." 2008. *Merriam-Webster Online Dictionary.* 25 April 2008 http://www.merriam-webster.com/ dictionary/wellspring.

"Blue Letter Bible." 2008. 25 May 2008, http://www. blueletterbible.org/.

Smalley, Gary and Trent, John PH.D. *The Gift of The Blessing.* Updated, expanded edition. Nashville: Thomas Nelson Publishers, 1993, p. 53.

"oxygen-review.com." 2009. 15 August 2009 http://www. oxygen-review.com/human-body.html.

Tozer, Aiden Wilson. *Tozer on the Holy Spirit.* Compiled by Marilynne E. Foster. Camp Hill: Christian Publications, Inc., 2000. April 25.

"talent." 2008. *Merriam-Webster Online Dictionary.* 20 August 2008 http://www.merriam-webster.com/ dictionary/talent.

"ability." 2008. *Merriam-Webster Online Dictionary.* 20 August 2008 http://www.merriam-webster.com/ dictionary/ability.

"abundant." 2008. *Merriam-Webster Online Dictionary.* 17 July 2008 http://www.merriam-webster.com/ dictionary/abundant.

Chambers, Oswald. *My Utmost for His Highest.* Edited by James Reimann. Updated Edition. Grand Rapids: Discovery House Publishers, 1992. May 18.

"Knights of the Round Table." 2009. *Wikipedia The Free Encyclopedia.* 25 August 2009 http://www.en.wikipedia. org/wiki/Knights_of_the_Round_Table.

Eldridge, John. *Wild at Heart.* Nashville: Thomas Nelson Publishers, 2001, pp. 171–172.